By The Editors Of Consumer Guide®

COMPLETE
BICYCLE
BOOK

BEEKMAN HOUSE
New York

Contents

Library of Congress Catalog Card Number: 80-80642
ISBN: 0–517–307812

This edition published by:
Beekman House
A Division of Crown Publishers, Inc.
One Park Avenue
New York, N.Y. 10016

Photo Credits: AMF, Florida Department of Commerce, Frostline Inc., Huffy Corporation, Mavic, Motobecane, Murray, Peugeot, Raleigh-Rampar, Ross, Schwinn Bicycle Co., Shimano American

Manufactured in the United States of America
1 2 3 4 5 6 7 8 9 10

Introduction

Bicycle booms have come and gone since before the turn of the century but sales seem brisk once more, if not staggering, as we enter the 1980s.

Inflation and recession have taken only a slight bite from the market. Far more importantly, the rising gasoline prices and rumors of fuel rationing continue to prompt people into walking or, when possible, bicycling instead of driving to the store, the office or the park on Sundays.

People who took up bicycling as a fad in 1973 and 1974 are by now convinced it is a healthful, enjoyable way to get from one point to another. These are the same people who will soon be crowding the bicycle shops again, this time seeking to upgrade their equipment, to buy a bicycle better suited to their primary cycling interests like touring, racing or pedaling around the block.

Then, too, there's a whole new generation of bicyclists—the young moto-cross fans—dirt-track bicycle racers out to win their share of the bronze, silver and gold.

No matter what the reason, bicycling is here to stay. And that's good news, indeed, for the average American.

Bicycling And Health

There are few people around today who would question the health-enhancing effects of bicycle riding. Since former President Dwight Eisenhower suffered his life-threatening heart attack back in 1955 and his coronary expert, Dr. Paul Dudley White, recommended bicycling as a way to prevent future attacks, Americans have accepted pedaling as a way to good health.

Of course, bicycling's healthful benefits weren't always acknowledged and, perhaps, for good reason. Back in the bicycle's first heyday—around the turn of the century—many physicians believed that the two-wheelers were absolute menaces to their patients' well being. And this may have been true. If you've ever seen an old wooden-wheeled "hobby horse" or the monster-like high-wheeler less-than-affectionately called "bone-shaker" in a museum, you can understand the medical community's concern.

Also, many nineteenth-century physicians worried about their bicycling patients running up a grueling thirst, which they might be tempted to slake with beer (commonly thought to cause kidney stones). And there was always the real concern that touring cyclists might attempt to satisfy their thirsts by drinking water from rural wells, some of which were tainted with typhoid, a result of unsanitary conditions prevalent in those days. Although much of the advice was well intended, it's not hard to smile at the medical practitioner who told bicycle riders to chew gum as they pedaled to ward off the temptation of sampling from strange wells.

As if that weren't enough of a deterrent, many turn-of-the-century medical authorities claimed bicycling could lead to a whole host of even worse maladies. These included nerve damage, insanity, skeletal deformities, hernia, enlarged veins, and a series of disorders described merely by linking the word "bicycle" with that part of the body supposedly affected the most—such as "bicycle hands," "bicycle wrists," "bicycle legs," etcetera.

It's not surprising that those who risked their physicians' wrath by bicycling across the countryside were usually men. Women were thought to be "unladylike" if they rode bicycles (after all, it's hard for a lady to pedal sidesaddle). And women, too, were alleged to suffer the most serious of physical ailments and deformities after even a limited amount of pedal-pushing.

The wide acceptance of bloomers by milady—as well as her lack of gullibility—eventually won out, though. Soon men as well as women were pedaling throughout the land. And lack of hard evidence to the contrary finally encouraged enlightened doctors to admit that perhaps cycling wasn't so very harmful after all. In fact, according to a few scandalous medical mavericks, it might even be healthful.

Of course, merely owning a bicycle won't do much for a person's health. Buying a fancy 10-speed lightweight machine may boost your ego, but if you leave it sitting in the garage 12 months out of the year, it's not going to boost your heart rate.

But if you actually *use* that 10-speed machine—or five-speed or three-speed or single-speed, for that matter—that's when you can expect to start reaping rewards.

It's hardly a well-kept secret that Americans need more exercise. We live in a push-button society that places little, if any, physical demand on our bodies. The average American can quite easily rise in the morning, jump in a car and drive 20 miles to work, pull into an underground garage, walk 15 feet to the elevator, ride to the fifth floor, walk 40 feet to the desk, and remain there until it's time to reverse the procedure at 4:30 in the afternoon.

Even on the weekends and on holidays, too many of us hop into the car to drive to the store, to church, to the park, to wherever—no matter how near or far. And those of us who elect to stay home often end up glued in front of the television. There's not much physical activity there. That's one of the reasons the American Medical Association (AMA) claims nearly half of all Americans over the age of 40 are seriously overweight. An alarming number of these people succumb prematurely to heart attacks.

The AMA has made several studies which show that individuals who are overweight and underactive run a

Turn-of-the-century physicians thought two-wheelers, such as this 1886 racer, were menaces to their patients' health.

much higher risk of heart attack than slim and active people. Moreover, if a person who is in good physical condition does suffer an attack, that person has a much better chance of survival than his fatter and more sedentary counterpart. It's a sobering fact that 55% of American deaths result from diseases of the heart and blood vessels—diseases brought on, in many cases, by obesity and inactivity.

A regular program of bicycling—whether alone or in a group, such as a family—can do a lot to change all that. And the sooner the program is begun, the better. Our children are pampered by an automated society. They are transported to and from school by car or bus. During the evenings and through the weekends they are mesmerized by the endless stream of television shows geared to appeal directly to them. Unless they mend their ways, these children will run the same risk of heart attacks that now threaten their parents.

Hippocrates, the father of medicine, expressed it best: "That which is used develops, and that which is not used wastes away." The heart is a pump built of muscle, and just like the muscles of the arms and legs, it gets soft and becomes inefficient when it's not worked hard enough. When the heart is strengthened through exercise, the entire body benefits—circulation of the blood improves and the organs and muscles work together more efficiently.

An Efficient Form Of Exercise

To be of any lasting benefit, exercise must be sustained. We've all heard stories of the "weekend warrior" who strains his body beyond all normal limits once each weekend and finally collapses. Even the infrequent jogger can do more harm than good to his heart. Yet, it's not surprising that the monotony of jogging or of routine calisthenics quickly sours the appetite for regular physical exercise. In order to be successful, an exercise program must be performed regularly. To exercise regularly, most people need the added incentive that comes when the exercise is fun.

That's the reason bicycling is the ideal light exercise—it's fun. It's much more pleasant than many other get-fit or stay-fit programs which can get boring. In addition, bicycle riding doesn't depend on raising enough players to have a game, like team sports. Nor does it require a continuing output of money to participate—as do tennis, raquetball, and handball. That means children have a ready source of recreation in bicycle riding that will continue beyond the school years, for as long as they own a bicycle. Adults can derive the physical benefits of exercise while, at the same time, they avoid the monotony of other physical fitness activities.

Before you undertake a program of regular physical exercise—whether bicycling or any other activity—be sure to see your doctor for a complete physical examination. Only he can tell how much activity is safe and beneficial for you, especially if you're advancing in years. Certainly, anyone with a heart problem should be cautious before engaging in strenuous physical exertion. Even people without heart difficulties should start slowly and build-up gradually to a more rigorous level of exercise.

If you need still more incentive to exercise regularly, the President's Council on Physical Fitness offers awards to individuals who pedal their bicycles consistently. To receive a bicycling award, a person must pedal a minimum of 400 miles on a bicycle of five gears or less or 600 miles on a bicycle with more than five gears during a period of four months or less. The award requirements stipulate, though, that no more than 12 miles in any one day can be credited to the total mileage for the over-five-gear category, and that no more than eight miles per day can be credited to those who pedal with a five-speed-or-fewer bicycle.

A personal log, application form, and other pertinent information are available from the Presidential Sports Award, P.O. Box 129, Radio City Station, New York, NY 10019. Upon completion of the required distance, the bicyclist can send in the log and a three-dollar fee and receive a certificate, pin, and jacket patch. It's not exactly like winning the gold medal in the Olympics—but it is a mark of achievement anyone should be proud of.

The purpose of the program, of course, is "to get more adults to become active participants in sports, rather than being content with a spectator's role," according to the Council. "The Council believes that the physical and mental benefits resulting from vigorous exercise contribute to personal health, appearance, and performance."

A Healthful Prescription

For many folks, bicycling not only helps keep them physically fit, but also provides therapy for a number of specific ailments. Regular riders have reported remarkable progress in their struggle against bad backs, respiratory congestion, and cardio-vascular problems; others claim that regular pedal-pushing has led to remissions from emphysema, lowered blood pressure, and improved recoveries from heart attacks.

Besides benefiting the body, bicycling can also aid the mind. Regular pedaling makes a significant contribution to psychological well-being by helping to relieve stress, hypertension, and mental fatigue. Many psy-

Bicycling is healthful at any age.

Regular cycling helps relieve mental fatigue and allows time for creative thought.

chiatrists prescribe bicycle riding as therapy for mentally disturbed patients, and sociologists feel that group riding helps introverted persons overcome timidity and self-consciousness. And many people who regularly have problems falling asleep at night find that bicycling for several miles in the early evening works better than any sleeping pill.

Yet, one need not suffer from a serious mental malady to profit from regular bicycle riding. Many executives became so fatigued by the pressure and tension of the business world that their work suffers and they age more quickly than normal. Specialists who have studied key executives recommend rigorous exercise to bring about renewed vigor. Dr. Paul Dudley White once stated that no one should sit still for more than an hour without standing up and moving about. While it's often inconvenient—if not impossible—for office workers, students, business executives, and technicians to exercise every hour of the day, anyone can go for a brisk evening bicycle ride.

The pace of modern urban living can be exhausting, as few people will deny, but bicycling can be a remarkable restorative. A bicycle allows a person to catch up, to recapture precious privacy, and to re-establish a balanced state of mind. Some people even find that their moments of solitude astride a bicycle not only relieve anxiety, but also allow them time for creative thought. It's not necessary, of course, to come up with any profound thoughts or earth-shaking formulas in order to reap the mental benefits of pedaling a bicycle. Escape from pressure and tension is sufficient reward.

The Time Is Now

Many folks who start to feel they need physical exercise follow that old line about sitting down until the feeling passes. Certainly if a person wants to avoid getting his body into the shape in which it should be, there are numerous excuses. Yet, those who recognize the urgency of getting into shape before those potentially crippling diseases strike are the ones who benefit the most.

Though there are certain conditions that cyclists must handle with care, there's really no valid excuse for not riding a bicycle each and every day of the year. Even those living in the Snowbelt States can continue pedaling during most days of the winter months. With a stationary exercise cycle, one can accomplish a daily cycling stint while listening to music or watching TV.

If your pedaling takes you to where the air is thin—say, 9,000 feet or higher altitude—you should be careful. Even though there's quite a bit of fine bicycle touring to be enjoyed in the high country, altitude sickness can bring on general lethargy accompanied by headache, insomnia, breathlessness, nausea, and loss of appetite. Acclimatization is the key. Plan a gradual and leisurely ascent, and then rest for a couple days after reaching your high-altitude destination to give your body time to adjust to the altitude.

Certainly, anyone with health problems (especially heart, lung, and blood pressure disorders) should consult a doctor before embarking on a bicycle trip to the high country. In the rareified air of a mountain top, the heart must work harder (increasing the pulse rate) in order to supply the body with oxygen-rich blood. Of course, you should always see a doctor—even if you don't have a health problem—before engaging in a new program of physical exercise.

Even during the winter months, one can keep fit with a stationary exercise cycle.

Pedaling Away The Pounds

There's an undeniable correlation between exercise and weight control. If an individual exercises restraint in his diet and exercises his body on a bicycle, he can lose excess poundage. In fact, assuming that you don't increase your food intake, you can lose up to 25 pounds annually by adding 30 minutes of moderate bicycling a day to your regimen.

The key to effective weight control is merely a matter of metabolic arithmetic: Maintain a balance between energy intake (food consumption) and energy output (physical activity). The average adult male burns up between 2,400 and 4,500 calories each day, depending upon how much exercise he performs. He can boost his daily food intake up to 6,000 calories without adding an ounce to his weight—if he pursues a program of rigorous physical activity. A 150-pound person, for example, riding a bicycle at 5½ miles an hour consumes 210 calories for each hour he pedals. If he pushes his speed to 13 miles an hour, he more than triples his rate of caloric expenditure to 660 calories an hour!

What you eat is as important as how much you eat when planning a diet that's complementary to bicycling and other forms of exercise. Pastries, deep-fried foods, chocolate, fatty meats, butter, and dairy products made from whole milk or cream are rich in saturated fats. Egg yolks, liver, and other organ meats are high in choles-terol. These foods tend to raise the cholesterol level of the blood and encourage the development of arteriosclerosis (hardening of the arteries), commonly thought to be the forerunner of heart attacks and strokes.

The Time Is Right For You

If you're still not convinced about bicycling's ability to give you a better body and mind, you're probably beyond hope. There are a few things in this world worth more to body and mind than bicycling—but only a few. Millions of Americans now pedaling their way to better health are living testimonials to this fact. A regular program of bicycle riding produces the following health benefits:

1. Enables people to accomplish more without tiring so easily.
2. Gives an increased zest for living and a greater resistance to stress and strain of daily life.
3. Helps keep weight close to the normal level for height and bone structure.
4. Markedly improves appearance through better posture and a slimmer, more muscular figure.
5. Often helps lower high blood cholesterol levels, reduce the risk of heart attack, and improve the chance of recovering from an attack.

So if you choose to bicycle primarily for fun, exercise, or practical transportation, the time is right to begin.

Cycling is a healthful and fun sport that can be enjoyed by the whole family.

How It Was

For the first time in more than 70 years, registered bicycles outnumbered registered motor vehicles within Madison, Wisconsin city limits, according to a 1978 city census. Not too surprisingly, the Madison experience is happening in small towns and cities around the country. Part of the reason is that Madison is a typical college town, with more than a fourth of its resident population consisting of students—notoriously fitness- and economy-minded.

Even in non-college towns, the rising cost of buying, servicing, and fueling motor vehicles and the ease and fun of bicycling is resulting in greater numbers of pedal-pushers than ever before.

Yet the battle between auto and bicycle is deeply rooted in American history. For a while around the turn-of-the-century, the bicycle appeared to be the primary vehicle of personal transportation. It was destined—or so it seemed—to take that honor away from the horse, which was more expensive to buy and maintain. In fact, so rosy was bicycling's future that such inventive and far-seeing men as Henry Ford, Glen Olds (father of the modern Oldsmobile), and George N. Pierce were bicycle mechanics long before they eventually began manufacturing cars. When motorized vehicles finally swelled in popularity, thanks mostly to Ford's use of assembly line construction techniques that brought auto costs down to the affordable range, bicycles were, alas, relegated to the realm of child's plaything.

Pedal Progress

Actually, the earliest bicycles resembled toys. In the late 1790s, a Frenchman named Comte de Sivrac constructed a crude wooden horse, mounted it on two

9

Bicycles outnumbered horses on the Chicago streets of 1897. (Courtesy of the Chicago Historical Society.)

wheels, and placed a padded saddle across the top. Sivrac's wooden horse had no front fork for steering, and there was no drive mechanism, which meant the rider had to push the vehicle along like a scooter; so it soon lost favor with the country folks.

Around 1816, Baron Karl Von Drais, the superintendent of forests in the city of Karlsruhe, Germany, developed a steerable two-wheeled vehicle called the "Draisine," or hobby horse. It helped Von Drais to move about on the forest paths during his many inspection tours. Legend says that he was able to make a 20-mile trip in three hours, even though locomotion was accomplished by pushing the vehicle with the feet on the ground, as in Sivrac's bicycle. In 1818, Von Drais took his invention to Paris, and a bicycle boom swept Europe. Nevertheless, poor road conditions, the machine's high cost, and the effort required to move the hobby horse across hilly terrain doomed it to oblivion.

Not until 1840 was there a two-wheeled vehicle that could be ridden with both feet off the ground. Kirkpatrick Macmillan, a successful Scottish blacksmith, developed a treadle-operated machine which marked the beginning of self-propelled cycles. Though Macmillan's machine promptly fell into obscurity, records indicate that the inventor proved the practicality of his device when he rode his bicycle on a 40-mile trip in 1842.

The next decades were relatively quiet where bicycles were concerned. Sometime during the 1860s, a Frenchman named Ernest Michaux placed pedals on the front axle, and the world greeted the birth of the "boneshaker." The Michaux invention consisted of

wooden wheels, iron tires, and a heavy iron frame. Riding a mechanism with this sort of construction, the cyclist had to be both strong and courageous. The boneshaker provided precisely the type of ride which its name implies.

While Michaux was an ingenious inventor, he wasn't a particularly adept businessman. On November 10, 1866, a disgruntled Michaux employee named Pierre Lalloment came to America and took out the first U.S. bicycle patent.

Meanwhile, back in France, Michaux produced about 400 of his machines in 1865, and manufacturers throughout the world subsequently made hundreds of improvements to the basic boneshaker. Because of its extreme awkwardness, weight, and maneuverability problems, the boneshaker lapsed into obsurity just as the Age of the Bicycle was beginning.

Around 1870, James Starley of Coventry, England, enlarged the size of the bicycle's front wheel, reduced the size the the back wheel, and offered the world what came to be known as the "ordinary." Since the rider was, for the first time, able to thrust his legs downward effectively, the ordinary is considered the first practical bicycle.

During the 1876 Centennial Exposition in Philadelphia, English manufacturers exhibited the ordinary to skeptical Americans. When the Exposition closed, the unsold ordinaries were purchased by the Cunningham Company, the first bicycle importing firm in the U.S. Shortly thereafter, the first bicycles to be manufactured in America went on the market under the Columbia

By 1896, bicycle touring had become a popular sport. (Courtesy of the Chicago Historical Society.)

trade name. The Columbia ordinary weighed more than 70 pounds and cost $313, a staggering amount of money for those times. But bicycle fever was rampant throughout the nation, and everyone who was anyone just had to own a Columbia.

Touring had become a popular sport in 1873 when four riders pedaled from London to the northern coast of Scotland, a distance of 800 miles, in 14 days. Not to be outdone, a Boston man named Thomas Stevens, riding for two years on an 1884 Columbia, became the first man to circumnavigate the globe on a two-wheeler. Stevens faced and surmounted incredible difficulties, including hostile Indians in his own country.

During the early 1870s, bicycling flourished despite the expense and risk of riding the ordinary. In 1870, the longest surviving club, The Pickwick Cycling Club, was founded in London. Soon bicyclists were taking to the roads in record numbers. Still, most roads were designed for and used by horses, and early bicycle tourists had to match wits against a variety of less-than-perfect cycling conditions.

If anything was clear from the days of the ordinary it was that man had decided he would bicycle. The perilous nature of the ordinary and the inventor's tenacious nature combined, by 1885, to produce the "safety." In that year, John Kent Starley developed a chain-driven rear-wheel vehicle called the "Rover." The Starley invention featured a diamond-shaped frame with equal-size wheels which had been gaining in popularity in both Europe and America. In 1898, the New Departure Company added a coaster brake to make cycling safe for the entire family. Only details distinguish the modern bicycle of today from Starley's Rover.

The first Rover had wheels about 30 inches in diameter and solid rubber tires. Pneumatic tires didn't come into widespread use until 1888 when John Boyd Dunlop patented a process he discovered while making

The 1870 'Ariel.'
(Courtesy of the Bicycle Institute of America.)

The 'Star' bicycle. (Courtesy of the Chicago Historical Society.)

The Columbia Light Roadster Safety, 1889. (Courtesy of the Chicago Historical Society.)

more comfortable tires for his son's tricycle. By 1892, the pneumatic tire was being manufactured by many firms and had become the standard in bicycle tires.

Racing Into Oblivion

With the introduction of the pneumatic tire, a whole new sport was created: bicycle racing. The first six-day bicycle race in America took place in New York's old Madison Square Garden in 1891. Champion racer "Plugger Bill" Martin pedaled over 1,466 miles during

The 1885 'Rover.' (Courtesy of the Bicycle Institute of America.)

the six-day event. Although few bicycle enthusiasts at the time realized the fact, however, a new invention was looming on the horizon that would push the bicycle aside as a vehicle for touring and racing. In fact, nearly every improvement designed for the bicycle soon was applied to the upstart automobile: pneumatic and cord tires, ball bearings, differential steering, seamless steel tubing, expansion brakes, and gearing systems. The influence of the bicycle on the earliest power-driven automobiles can be seen easily. Some early autos look like little more than motorized tricycles!

Still, it wasn't only the car that drew upon bicycle technology. Two young brothers living in Dayton, Ohio, in 1892 opened their own bicycle sales and repair shop. After reading about the glider experiments of Otto Lilienthal in Germany and Octave Chanute in America, they grew interested in manufacturing and testing aircraft. In December, 1903, Orville and Wilbur Wright turned the world upside down with their first successful motorized aircraft flight.

Just one year earlier, young Henry Ford was seeking publicity for his new horseless carriage. He turned to colorful bicycle racing champion Barney Oldfield. Oldfield, who thrived on speed and was eager to race Ford's 80-horsepower "Old 999," won his first automobile race. Oldfield's sudden abandonment of the bicycle in favor of the upstart automobile symbolized the car's new-found dominance that would continue for the next three-quarters of a century.

By 1900, bicycling was the fashionable rage. (Courtesy of the Chicago Historical Society.)

The Bicycle's Revival

It wasn't until the 1950s that adults once again thought about the bicycle as a means of pleasurable transportation. During the previous 50 years, bicycles were strictly considered children's toys, or—at best—tools of the trade of newspaper and delivery boys.

Improvements in the machines, themselves, contributed greatly to the revived public interest in bicycling. During the early 1960s, the public discovered decent, rideable (usually imported) bicycles at affordable prices. Gone were the heavy, clumsy two-wheelers with fat tires that made pedaling a chore rather than a pleasure. Instead, there was a new-fangled European three-speed lightweight "racing bike" that allowed riders to break out of riding just around the neighborhood and permitted them to pedal out on 5- to 10-mile jaunts.

By the early 1970s, as problems of fuel and pollution began to seep into the minds of auto-conscious Americans, the bike boom grew to enormous magni-tudes, with new bicycle sales surpassing even new car sales. By now both domestic and imported bicycles were incredibly efficient machines, commonly equipped with three, five, or 10 speeds. These lightweight bicycles were designed to take a rider nearly anyplace he wanted to go. And the places riders wanted to go kept pace with the technological improvements in the machines themselves.

Commuting on a bicycle in good weather became a common sight in the nation's most congested urban areas, and the demand for bicycle byways and pathways replaced the demand for new super-highways in city council chambers around the country. Family vacations often began quite traditionally by car, then switched to bicycle as more and more people became familiar with the joys of seeing America close-up and outdoors.

As Americans move into the 1980s, bicycles have become more entwined in their lifestyle than has been the case for nearly a century.

Bicycles are again a common sight in the nation.

Selecting A Bicycle

Mention the word, bicycle, and today, the first thing people think of is a modern 10-speed tourer. Just a decade ago, the word conjured up images of a single-speed, balloon-tired contraption mostly ridden by kids and senior citizens.

Well, times change, but good things don't. The balloon-tire bike is still with us, still being manufactured and bought, still meeting the needs of a great many cyclists, both children and adults, alike. It seems the balloon-tire bike—as well as its sleeker, 10-speed cousin—will be around forever.

But they aren't the only types of bicycles in vogue. Several others include the three-speed (sometimes called an English racing bicycle, though it's anything but), the five-speed, the 12-speed, and the 15-speed. Within these different gearing groups are various special-use bicycles, such as moto-cross (usually single-speed dirt racing machines for children), tandem (which may vary from single-to-15-speed cycles), and adult tricycles (which, likewise, may vary in the number of speeds available). As you might have guessed by now, selecting the proper bicycle for you or your child is anything but child's play.

The first thing prospective buyers should be asked when they walk into a bicycle shop is, "What will you use the bicycle for?" It would be foolish for a competitive racer or long-distance tourer to buy a single-speed balloon-tire bike—equally so for an urban delivery or paper

boy to choose a lightweight $500 touring bicycle. To help you decide how many speeds you're likely to need for the type of riding you intend to do, here's a list of bicycles based upon their gearing systems and how they're most often used.

Single-Speed. This is most often used on level ground over short distances, ideally on paved urban roadways. Most single-speed bicycles are extremely heavy and, thus, durable.

Three-Speed. This functions well in most inner-city situations and in moderately hilly terrain for short distances. It's also a good bicycle for a youngster too old for single-speed bikes and too young to handle a more complex multi-speed machine. The lowest gear on the three-speed hub can negotiate small hills fairly easily.

Five-Speed. This bicycle can handle most commonly encountered terrain in touring and reduces pedaling effort on short trips.

Ten- or Twelve-Speed. The most popular and versatile gearing manufactured today, this cycle is used widely for exercise, recreational rides, touring, and road racing over all but the most severe terrain. It enables riders to travel long distances with relatively little effort.

Fifteen-Speed. This wide-range gearing bicycle is used primarily by those tourers who cycle over very hilly terrain and for exceptionally long distances. It's available in extra-low "Alpine" gears which are used mostly for cycling in mountainous areas.

Once you've decided what type gearing you need in a bicycle, buying the right cycle for you should be easy, right? Wrong. At least if you care about getting the most value for your money. Within these wide gearing groupings, many different brands and models exist. Each of these models varies slightly in engineering and design, construction techniques, and materials. Perhaps nowhere is this difference more apparent—or more critical—than in the bicycle's frame.

The Frame

The frame has been called the heart of the bicycle, and rightly so. For it's the frame that provides stability, accepts the stress and strain of riding over smooth surfaces as well as bumpy ones, and generally holds the various other component parts together. How the frame is made—and the type of material from which it is constructed—is crucial to the overall quality of the bicycle.

Bicycle frames are constructed of many different types of metal and tubing. Less expensive bicycles usually feature frames made of seamed tubing, which means a flat strip of steel is wrapped into a tubular form by rollers and then automatically welded to form a tube. This tube is called "straight gauge," because it's not reinforced where it joins the other parts of the bike. Usually, where one of these straight-gauge tubes meets another, the two are simply welded together or the one is stuck into a hole drilled in the other and then the joint is welded electrically.

Today, there's a bike made for every rider's needs.

This method of construction can lead to problems, because the electric weld is made at extremely high temperatures, which can result in a weakening of the metal. The finished frame isn't likely to hold up to the

The lightweight 10- and 12-speed bicycles are the most popular with adult riders.

A weak frame construction. The rear dropout is stamped metal, stuck and welded into pressed steel side stays.

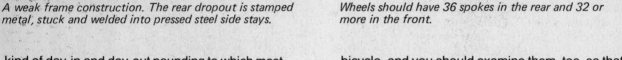

Wheels should have 36 spokes in the rear and 32 or more in the front.

kind of day-in and day-out pounding to which most bicycles are subjected.

At the other end of the spectrum, the best bicycle frames are made of double-butted, cold-drawn, seamless manganese-and-molybdenum steel. This type of tubing can withstand rough handling and is yet light enough to resist fatigue. It has a high tensility for maximum resilience without being too springy.

While it's difficult to tell if a frame is double-butted by looking at it, those bicycle manufacturers who use this type of tubing will advertise it. (Double butting means that the metal is thicker at both ends of the tube where the maximum amount of stress occurs. Yet, the outside diameter of the tube is unchanged.)

Also, while many manufacturers use double-butted manganese-molybdenum steel frames on their more expensive models, not all assemble the frames the same way. Reynolds, a leader in producing steel for bicycle frames, specifies that the welding should be done by hand using a low-temperature (850 degrees Centigrade or less as opposed to the 1,400 degrees or more some manufacturers use) bronze brazing material for the strongest possible frame. For more strength still, frames should be "lugged." Where one tube of the frame meets another, a lug—a small metal sleeve into which the tubes fit prior to brazing—should appear. A lugged frame can be easily identified from an unlugged frame. For the best possible bicycle frame, look for the words, "All-lugged, low-temperature, bronze-brazed," or something similar.

Of course, not all cyclists—even the experts—choose such frames for their own bicycles. While all-lugged, molybdenum steel alloy frames are the most durable, they're also heavier than some other frame types. Racers and long-distance tourers, concerned equally with weight and durability, would rather have an unlugged frame construction of extremely lightweight metal alloy, like aluminum. Again, the use to which the bicycle will be put should play the determining factor in the selection of the bicycle frame.

There are several other components comprising any bicycle, and you should examine them, too, so that you know exactly what you're getting for your money.

Rims. The finest rims available today are usually made of an aluminum alloy. Steel rims are heavier and generally indicate a lower quality bike. Aluminum rims are also durable, although they're not impervious to bending or even breaking if mistreated, so some care should be taken. Steel rims are often standard fare on children's bikes.

Hubs. Campagnolo hubs are regarded as the highest quality available, though Normandy, Cinelli, and Simplex are all good brands. These are constructed of one-piece machined aluminum. Avoid the stamped-metal hub. Quick-release hubs feature hollow axles that allow a quick-release rod to pass through the hub to lock both sides to the bicycle's fork. Quick-release hubs (sometimes denoted as "QR") are generally more expensive, but seem worth the investment, as the wheels are easy to release in seconds (and without tools!) for ease and speed in changing a flat tire or performing other work on the wheel.

Wheels. These should have 36 spokes in the rear wheel and 32 or more in the front as standard fare. English three-speed bicycles usually have 40 spokes rear and 32 front, and some lightweight models have 36 spokes both front and rear. A few smaller-sized bicycles (with 24-inch wheels or smaller) feature 28 spokes both front and rear. If a wheel has fewer than the number of spokes listed above, it's likely to be weak and could cause trouble under pressure. All spokes should be double-butted (thicker at both ends than in the middle).

Lugs. As mentioned earlier, lugs are sleeves of metal that act as braces where one tube of the frame joins another. One of the highest regarded lugs is manufactured by Nervex.

Derailleurs. These magnificent pieces of technology make multi-speed bicycles possible. They allow for quick, generally error-free changing of gears from one to 15 (and, theoretically at least, beyond). By far, the best quality and most expensive are made by Campagnolo. The Nuovo Record is generally regarded as

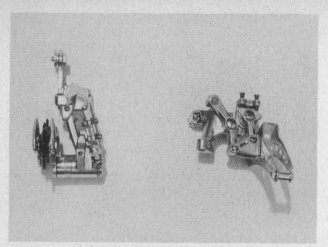

Derailleurs make quick, error-free change of gears possible on multi-speed bicycles.

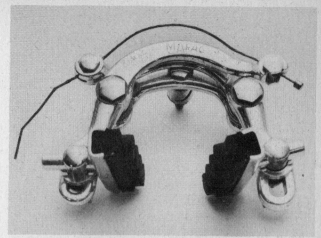

Quality center-pull brakes from a reputable manufacturer provide reliable stopping ability.

"Campy's" very best, followed by the Gran Sport. Simplex' Prestige is also a fine quality derailleur, as are Huret's Allvit and Shimano's Altus LT Deluxe.

Cranks and Chainwheel Assemblies. Where would a bicycle be without a crank and chainwheel? Back to the days of the old boneshakers! Once again, Campagnolo manufactures the best, called the Record Strada, followed by the Stronglight and Williams. The best cranks and chainwheels are made from aluminum

alloy, forged and cotterless. Cottered cranks use a key to hold the steel crank on the crank axle and are generally considered standard fare on a lower quality bicycle.

Brakes. Here, opinion on the best is divided. The least expensive caliper brakes are side-pull models that offer more headaches than advantages. Inexpensive side-pulls may grip the rims unevenly, causing poor stopping ability and perhaps endangering the cyclist. At the top of the line, well-designed center-pull brakes and quality constructed side-pulls share an equal number of fans. The best brakes, whether center-pull or side-pull models, are made from aluminum alloy and allow for brake shoe adjustment. Two respected brand names are Mafac and Weinmann, though Campagnolo also makes an excellent side-pull.

Tires. The most expensive and highest quality bicycles usually feature 27-inch wheels and tubular (sew-up or tubeless) road-racing tires. But tube-type 27 × 1¼-inch tires are commonly used and are probably more popular with novice-to-intermediate cyclists. Though tubular sew-ups are more likely to go flat in inner-city bicycling and are somewhat more difficult to repair because the casing is sewn-up all the way around the tire, they are generally lighter in weight than tube-type wire-on tires and the wheels they are used on. That's an important consideration for racers and long-distance tourers where every additional ounce can be crucial. Also, tubular sew-ups can be changed in seconds and are so light that several spares can be carried along (the damaged tubulars may be repaired later at a more convenient time). Tube-type tires, on the other hand, are more time-consuming to change but easier to repair on the spot because of the accessability to the inner tube.

Pedals. Once again, Campagnolo pedals are generally regarded as being at the head of the class. The Lyotard platform pedal, too, is excellent—both sturdy and less expensive than the Campy pedal.

Handlebars. Though many novice cyclists instinctively shy-away from drop-type handlebars because of

Aluminum alloy cotterless cranks and chainwheels are found on more expensive bicycle models.

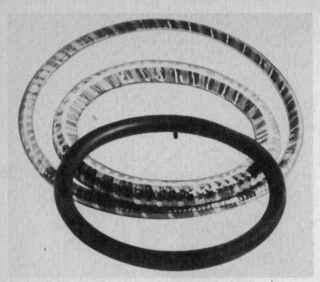

Depending on your needs, you may choose either tubular or tubeless (sew-up) tires.

the "awkward" position they place the body in, they are really the best type bars for nearly all types of bicycling. To ride a bike with dropped bars, the cyclist has to crouch down at about a 45-degree angle to the ground, cutting down on wind resistance (thus saving pedaling energy). Also, with the hunched-back position, the cyclist can use more muscles more effectively over a longer period of time than when cycling with a bike equipped with upright bars.

If you're not convinced, try this simple at-home demonstration. Sitting upright in a straight-backed chair (the way you'd sit on a bicycle with upright handlebars), try standing. Notice the amount of strain this simple action places on your body. Next, sit in the chair and bend forward at about 45 degrees. As you stand from this position, notice how much easier it is to rise. That's because you've positioned your body weight forward so you can rely more on your strong back and thigh muscles. Translated to bicycling, this means you'll have greater cycling efficiency with less energy expended

when riding a dropped-bar bike.

Of course, choosing a bicycle featuring the very best component parts may not always be practical, unless money is no object. But many bicycle components are interchangeable, and it's often possible to request other-than-standard derailleurs or rims, for example, when making a purchase. As in buying a new car, you must choose the parts you want balanced against the money you have to spend. In general, if you buy the best bicycle you can possibly afford, you'll be happy for years to come. There's no bicycle that's more expensive than a cheaply constructed one. A bargain-basement brand could cost you time and fun while the cycle sits in the repair shop and may even be dangerous—the most important consideration.

Where To Buy

Where you buy your bicycle is nearly as important as the type of machine you finally select. It is recommended you consider only reputable bicycle stores. Though you may save a few dollars by buying the same or a similar bicycle at a discount or department store, the savings are sure to be negated in the long run. Here's why.

Bicycle manufacturers ship their products to dealers around the country with component parts unassembled. Handlebars, pedals, brakes, derailleurs, seat, fenders, and required safety reflectors may all be uninstalled. Also, adjusting all parts to the proper size and function remains to be done. If you buy a disassembled bicycle in a carton, you're stuck with all that work—and you're asking for trouble. If you rely on some salesperson to assemble the bike in the backroom of the store, you're relying on luck.

Most bicycle manufacturers furnish a stringent set of rules and guidelines for their authorized bicycle dealers' technicians to follow when assembling their various models, along with another set of specifications for critical adjustments to derailleurs, brakes, etc. Few department store assemblers can or will follow such guidelines.

Even "fully assembled" and cartoned bicycles bought

Dropped (or racing) style handlebars.

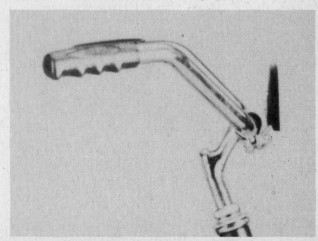

Upright (or tourist) style handlebars.

Choose the right bicycle for your child to ensure safe and happy riding.

at a discount house can be a disappointment. Many come with protective gum tape on the frame and fenders, uninstalled gear-shift handles and cables, uninstalled fenders and handlebars, and unadjusted seats. Furthermore, you're likely to find broken or loose spokes, incorrectly set caliper brakes, and binding hubs, forks, and bearing bracket cones. Are you willing to tackle all that work required in order to save $15 or $20?

In order for a bicycle to be properly fitted to the rider, it must be adjusted by an expert—a procedure that can take an hour or longer. (See the chapter, "Fitting A Bicycle Properly"). Proper fit is crucial to safe, easy bicycling. Buying a bike in a box is simply taking "pot luck."

Bikes For Children

There are several rules you should follow when choosing a bicycle for a growing child. One that applies across the board is to buy a frame that fits! Oversized bicycles bought in the belief that the child will "grow into" them are not only frustrating for the child to ride, but also dangerous. It's easy for a youngster to lose control of a bicycle that's too large. On a busy street, that could mean tragedy.

Also do not buy a young child a bicycle with multiple gears and with hand-lever caliper brakes. He won't have the strength or patience to operate them.

For children from five to seven years of age, a bicycle with a 10–20-inch wheel is recommended. For seven to ten year olds, choose a 24-inch wheel with coaster brakes. For 10-to-12 year-olds, a 26-inch wheel with perhaps a three-speed rear hub and front-and-rear caliper brakes. For an older child still, you might consider a 26-inch wheel with thinner "touring" type tires, although if the bicycle will be hauling heavy loads (groceries, newspapers, etc.), the larger 1¾-inch tires will take the extra weight better.

No matter what the child's age, make sure the bicycle is equipped with front and rear lights for after-dusk cycling, even if only on the sidewalk out in front of the house. A generator-type light eliminates the need for batteries and ensures there'll be light available when needed most.

Remember, just as in buying a bicycle for yourself, choose a child's model that's the best you can afford. With seat and handlebar adjustment, a good bicycle will last even the fastest growing child from four to six years. A poorly constructed machine, though, may have to struggle to make it through even a single cycling season.

Fitting A Bicycle Properly

Buying a bicycle isn't quite the same as buying other consumer products. When you buy a new appliance, car or movie camera, you're concerned only with the intrinsic quality of the article itself. When you buy a bicycle, you must consider not only the machine, but also the fit of the frame, saddle, and handlebar. The finest quality bicycle will be hard to handle and dangerous to ride if it's too large or too small for you.

In addition, there's no reason you must ride an improperly fitted bicycle. Most manufacturers offer a wide range of frame sizes with appropriate handlebar stems and seat posts providing a great deal of latitude in individual adjustment. Remember, though, that most bike shops only stock a small number of sizes in any given model. If your favorite model doesn't fit you, either shop around until you find the model you want in the

proper size, change to a proper fitting model that is in stock, or place a special order for your favorite model in the proper size.

What constitutes a good fit? Before answering that question, you should know something about the three bicycle components that largely determine your pedaling comfort and performance: frame, saddle, and handlebar. Once you select these items in the right style and size for you, you'll experience the thrill of riding a finely tuned machine.

The Frame

Everyone knows that there are bicycles designed primarily for men and women; but in this liberated age, it's not at all unusual to see a woman pedaling a man's bicycle (though the reverse isn't common—and for good reason, as we'll see). Actually, there are many reasons for everyone riding a man's style bike. It is stronger and presents fewer problems in the fitting of cables and accessories. Since it's stronger and more rigid, it is less prone to oscillations (or frame whip) when subjected to hard riding; that translates to better overall handling.

A ladies' style frame is neither as strong nor as precise in handling as a men's style. Racers of both sexes, for instance, ride the men's diamond frame bicycles; and an increasing number of all women pedalers are opting for the triangular men's bike construction. So why do manufacturers continue to offer the ladies' style frame? Primarily for cultural reasons. The ladies' frame style survives as a tribute to the past. It was originally designed with its angled top tube in deference to feminine modesty around the turn of the century. The purpose was to allow a woman to mount, ride, and dismount demurely. But in this day and age, when few women wear anything but jeans, shorts, or slacks while pedaling, the women's style is simply obsolete. Unless women plan to undertake long rides in flowing skirts, they shouldn't feel bashful about buying a man's style bicycle.

For the woman not interested in pedaling a men's style bicycle, though, a compromise frame is available by some manufacturers. It's called the mixte frame, and it's a modified version of the ladies' style frame with a higher top tube for more stability. An attempt to combine the best of both worlds in bicycle frame design, the mixte provides easy mounting and dismounting, along with a somewhat superior ride to the traditional ladies' style. Since only a few European manufacturers produce mixte bicycle frames, however, you may have some difficulty locating one in the right size for you.

The Saddle

Bicycle saddles, like other two-wheeler components, are more complicated than most novices realize. Saddles come in two basic styles, and the differences are significant. The mattress (or tourist) saddle is soft, blunt-nosed, well padded and sprung, and generally made of plastic or similar synthetic material. In contrast, the racing saddle (which actually has little to do with racing, other than the fact that virtually all bicycle racers choose this design) is firm, more pointed in the nose, without much (or any) padding and springs, and usually made entirely of leather or a leather covering over a plastic base.

Over the years many bicycle buyers have turned their noses up at racing saddles. Beginning riders often accuse them of being far inferior to the mattress saddle from the standpoint of comfort. Novices wonder aloud why they should be forced to sit on a narrow and hard seat when they could be astride the pillow-like touring saddle. Yet, there really are some excellent reasons to choose the racing saddle over its plusher counterpart.

If your bicycle racing consists of short jaunts within the neighborhood, you'll probably never realize the superiority of the all-leather saddle. On longer rides, though, the synthetic base and padding of the tourist

The ladies' mixte-style frame and the standard men's frame.

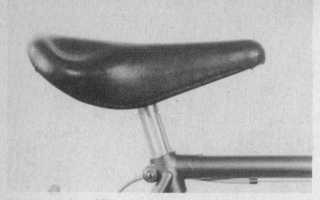

A racing-style saddle.

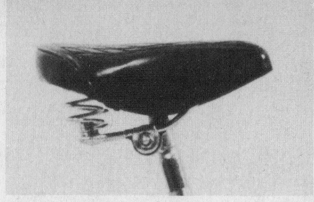

A tourist-style saddle.

saddle can trap heat, and the large blunt contours can chafe the inside of your legs. Each time you shift your body weight to pedal, you may also hear the annoying squeak of a tourist saddle's springs.

The racing saddle, on the other hand, gradually softens, molding its shape to match yours, with use. What starts out as a hard, stiff seat soon becomes as comfortable as an old pair of shoes—and for good reason. Just like leather shoes, racing saddles are made to be broken in slowly. Given enough time and care, the leather grows around you. Racing saddles that are partly synthetic require a shorter break-in period, and are quite satisfactory for most riders.

All-leather racing saddles do require extra attention and care. Periodically, you should give the racing saddle a complete overhaul with some type of leather treatment. And, while you can get away with such cavalier treatment as leaving a tourist saddle out in the rain, scratching or scuffing it, or even allowing grease or oil spatters to settle on it, an all-leather racing saddle is absolutely unforgiving. If you weigh these debits, though, against the merits of minimal leg chafing—especially on longer cycling trips and tours—easy pedaling action, and general riding comfort once broken in, you'll probably come out on the side of the all-leather racing saddle.

The Handlebar

Once you decide on frame and saddle design, you'll be faced with the next major design affecting fit—handlebar design. As a rule, if you've opted for the tourist (mattress) saddle, you should have a tourist (or upright) handlebar. Conversely, choosing the racing saddle dictates that you also select the racing (or dropped) handlebar style. This is because tourist saddles are designed to be most comfortable while sitting generally upright, while racing saddles are designed to be most comfortable while bent at approximately a 45-degree angle to vertical. As you might imagine, the two different styles don't mix well, while the tourist saddle and upright handlebar—as well as the racing saddle and dropped bar—are complementary.

The traditional upright handlebar is acceptable for

very short rides, but as we discussed earlier, it can cause numbness and tingling on the palms over long distances. Since the tourist handlebar offers no provision for changing hand positions, it must be adjusted precisely to the rider's requirements. Even then, it's likely to be uncomfortable over the long haul. Moreover, the upright bar demands that you sit in a position that can create considerable aerodynamic drag, and it also prevents the rider from exerting maximum leverage on the pedals.

The dropped handlebar is always the choice of the serious cyclist. The drop style, curving downward and to the rear, provides several different locations for your hands: the straight top portion, the curved portion, the part directly behind the brake lever placement, or the straight bottom portion of the bar. There's never a problem in finding a new place to put your hands and thereby break the monotony of using a single set of muscles. In addition, the hunched-down riding position lowers the center of gravity, increases overall stability, and allows better use of both calf and thigh muscles, as well as the powerful back muscles, for superior leverage on the pedals.

Fitting Procedures

Once you've decided on a frame, saddle, and handlebar style, it's time to begin the actual fitting procedures. While many of these procedures should be practiced by a knowledgeable bicycle salesperson at the time you buy your bicycle, it's imperative that you, too, are familiar with them so that you can check to see that the bicycle does, indeed, fit the intended rider.

The range of standard bicycle sizes extends from 17 to 26 inches, with the most common being 20 to 23 inches. These designations are meant to correlate with your inside leg measurement (the inseam) from the crotch to the bottom of your stocking feet. The rule of thumb is that you take your inseam, subtract nine inches, and the resulting number corresponds to the right frame size for you. Generally speaking, this measuring technique is reliable, although there are some exceptions.

The first actual fitting procedure is to straddle the bike

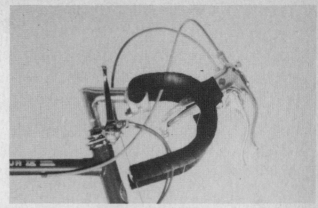

Tourist-style (or upright) handlebars.

Racing-style (or drop) handlebars.

of your choice to make sure that there's ample clearance between you and the top bar—from ½ to 1 inch. If you can't straddle the top tube comfortably, with both feet flat on the ground, go to a smaller frame size. If, on the other hand, there's more than an inch clearance, try the next larger frame size. Never try to compensate for the wrong size frame by raising or lowering the saddle. Too small a frame will make you feel cramped with the seat at normal height; raising the seat will place you in an awkwardly high-from-the-frame position. Too large a frame can be hard to handle and unsafe to ride.

Finding the proper frame size shouldn't be a problem for most people, but that's only the first step in getting a proper fit. Once you find a bicycle that seems right, you can then begin a more precise fitting.

Loosen the bolt that secures the seat post in the seat mast of the frame and raise or lower the saddle to the correct height. Proper saddle height is determined by sitting on the saddle and placing your feet on the pedals. There should be a very slight bend of the knee with the

pedal at the lowest downstroke and you sitting squarely on the saddle with the ball of your foot flush against the pedal.

Most likely, you'll feel a bit uncomfortable with the saddle raised to the proper height. Many riders, in fact, have their saddles set too low. Stick with your initial fit for at least 50 miles of cycling. Then, if you're still uncomfortable, make only very gradual adjustments of saddle height. Minute changes can make a vast difference in pedaling efficiency and enjoyment.

Be sure that you don't raise the saddle too high, or you'll be asking for trouble. Always leave at least two inches of seat post remaining within the seat mast of the frame. The seat post undergoes a great deal of stress while riding, and if there's less than two inches of it inside the seat tube, the post could snap and strand you without a saddle—not a very pleasing state. Since most seat posts don't have a maximum height indication, make your own mark on the post at two inches above its end, and never raise the saddle above that marking. It's

PROPER RIDER ADJUSTMENT

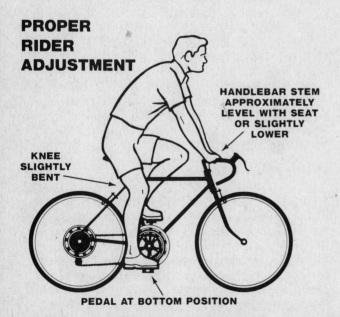

HANDLEBAR STEM
APPROXIMATELY
LEVEL WITH SEAT
OR SLIGHTLY
LOWER

KNEE
SLIGHTLY
BENT

PEDAL AT BOTTOM POSITION

PROPER FRAME FIT

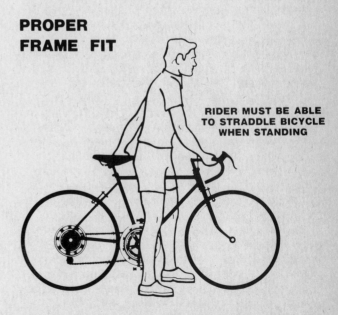

RIDER MUST BE ABLE
TO STRADDLE BICYCLE
WHEN STANDING

Fitting your bicycle properly: At least two inches of both the seatpost and handlebar stem must remain inside the frame and fork stem after adjustments are made.

A bicycle must fit properly to be safe. You must have at least half an inch of clearance at the top tube (A) with your feet flat on the ground. The seat height (B) should allow the rider's leg to be completely extended when the pedal is at its lowest point. The distance between the saddle and the crank (C) should correspond to your inseam measurement. Drop style handlebars (D) should tilt downward at about 10 degrees.

also a good idea to mark the seat post at the proper height for you and to check it periodically before taking the bicycle out to be sure the nut hasn't loosened and the saddle slipped down.

The handlebar stem should be approximately level with the saddle. The stem serves to connect the handlebar to the frame, and, like the seat post, the handlebar stem should never be raised too high. If there's less than 2½ inches of the stem in the head tube, you risk having the stem break off in your hands during hard riding. No handlebar stem, of course, means no steering.

To raise the stem so that the bar is parallel with the saddle, loosen the stem bolt and tap it lightly with a small mallet until the stem is freed. Position the bar at the correct height and tighten the stem bolt fully. Then mark the stem at the point where it meets the tube, loosen the bolt and remove the stem, and measure the amount of stem between the mark and the start of the stem skirt split. If the measurement is less than 2½ inches, buy a longer stem.

You will also need a different size stem if your arm measurement is much different than the distance between saddle and handlebar. The distance should be roughly equal to the length of your lower arm measured from the fingertips to the elbow. You must, of course, be able to reach the bar without straining. If you can't do so, the stem is too long for you.

Alternate stems are available at a modest price.

Having the proper size stem is well worth the investment. On the other hand, considerable labor is required to change the stem. The handlebar and at least one brake lever, as well as the tape (if present) on one side of the bar, must be removed. Therefore, make sure a change is necessary before you decide to tackle the job of switching handlebar stems.

The handlebar position within the stem must also be correct. Dropped handlebars should be tilted at an angle of about 10 degrees toward the ground. To make the adjustment, loosen the stem bolt, rotate the bar until the grip portion points down at a 10-degree angle to the ground, and re-tighten the stem bolt. Tourist handlebars should be positioned so that the ends point to the rear and slightly down.

Fitting A Child's Bicycle

Bicycles for children under 13 years of age require the same type of adjustments as do adult models, but there are a few other rules to follow when fitting a bike to a child.

The biggest problem parents make when buying a bike for a son or daughter is purchasing a model that's either too large or too complex. Often, the child is at least partly to blame, as he wants a bicycle "just like mom's" or "just like dad's." While all parents want to satisfy their children, giving in to a child's desires in

The right fit on a child's bicycle is important for safe riding. The child should have at least half an inch of clearance at the top tube (A) with his feet flat on the ground. The seat height (B) should allow the rider's leg to be completely extended when the pedal is at its lowest point. The distance between the saddle and the crank should correspond to the child's inseam measurement. Upright handlebars (D) should be positioned so that they point toward the rear and slightly down.

bicycles may make the youngster miserable. The bicycle may be too large or hard to pedal easily. If the frame is too large, he won't be able to mount or dismount safely. He'll be quite unhappy, too, if his feet dangle an inch or so above the pedals at the downstroke, and building-up the pedals with wooden blocks and bolts can be dangerous.

Also, a bike must be simple enough for a child to control safely and easily. Gearshifts and caliper brakes look fancy enough, but they may lead to problems. A young rider must be able to reach the brake mechanism and operate it efficiently. Frequently, children can't reach handlebar-mounted levers, or else they don't yet have the strength to squeeze the levers hard enough for swift, smooth stopping. Also, many young children have enough to worry about in keeping their balance; introducing complex gears and brakes will just frustrate them all the more and turn what should be a joyful experience into a real headache. Why risk spoiling a lifetime of cycling enjoyment by increasing the potential for serious accidents?

After you've made all appropriate adjustments for a precise fit, check all nuts and bolts to make sure they're fully tightened. If you find you can twist the saddle, handlebar, or handlebar stem, simply re-tighten the appropriate nut or bolt. If the saddle or handlebar still moves, place a drop of oil on the nut or bolt and tighten again. There may have been some binding present.

Next, sight down over the handlebar toward the front hub axle. The handlebar should be properly aligned in relation to the front fork; the straight top portion of the handlebar should be parallel with the front hub axle.

Make the same sort of final inspection and adjustments on all bicycles, but remember that kids tend to be rougher on their bikes than adults are. Check all nuts and bolts on a regular basis—once every month during peak riding season isn't too often—and make sure all equipment is still operating and properly adjusted.

Ready To Use

When you're riding a bicycle that's precisely fitted, you experience the thrill of operating a finely tuned machine that's as close to being one with your body as possible. Before long, you'll feel that your bicycle is an extension—and a highly responsive one—of your own self. Muscles are used to full advantage, and the bicycle's controls are within easy reach for top efficiency.

At first, you may not fully appreciate these settings. Remember to give them a chance, especially if you're new to modern bicycling. After pedaling for at least 50 miles, change the saddle and handlebar position if you're uncomfortable, but make only gradual alterations. You'll find that a tiny fraction of an inch difference in saddle or handlebar height can make a world of difference in your pedaling pleasure.

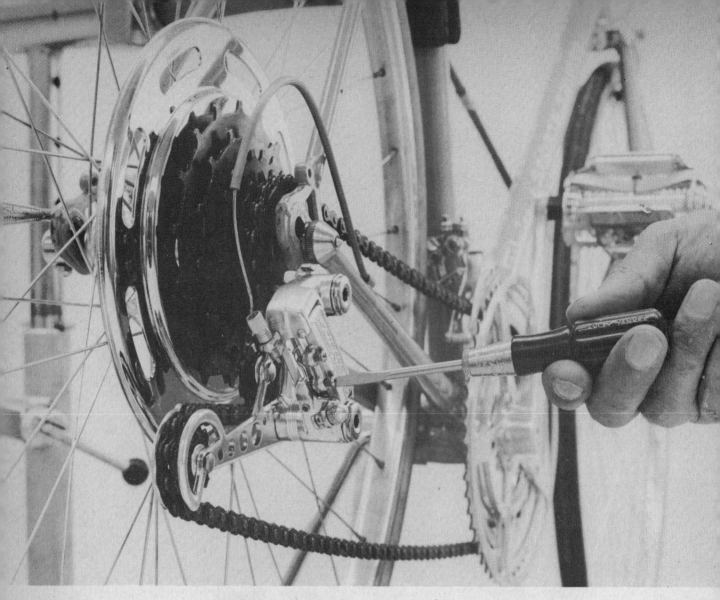

Maintenance And Repairs

You wouldn't dream of buying a new car and running it for years and years without periodic tune-ups, oil level checks, and the like. That's because you realize that, with just a little preventive medicine, you can keep your car healthy and running for many years without major difficulties.

It's much the same with a bicycle. Some people ride their bicycles for two or three years—even longer—without so much as a thought toward adjusting brake cables or greasing the chain or axle. And when everything starts breaking down at once, they curse the manufacturer for not building a product that lasts. Then it's too late for preventive maintenance. Either they must invest a hefty sum in a complete overhaul or

trade the bike in on a brand new model.

Considering the little amount of time and energy required to keep a bicycle functioning properly, there's really no excuse for letting it run down—especially when you consider the fact that an out-of-tune bike can endanger your safety. Yet, proper care will enable your bicycle to last for years without ever seeing the inside of a repair shop.

When you think of maintenance, you probably think of a dull routine that threatens to encroach on your Sunday afternoon with the family. And it can be that way. However, if you think of maintenance in terms of TLC (tender loving care), and if you arm yourself with a little knowledge and a few important tools, it will be easier and more rewarding to periodically tackle the job of maintaining your bike.

Besides tender loving care, TLC in bicycling means Tightening, Lubrication, and Cleaning. Give your bicycle just a bit of that each season, and you'll be in for years of relatively carefree—as well as safe and enjoyable—cycling.

The cyclist who cares for his bicycle will do all the routine chores out of love because he wants his bike to be a source of continuing pleasure. Whether you "love" your bicycle or would just love to hang onto your money, there are ways to turn routine maintenance into automatic, painless care.

Routine Checks

First of all, there are some things you should check whenever you ride your bicycle. These are not checks that require putting the bike on a maintenance rack. They're usually done as you ride. Soon, they'll become second nature, like pedaling or steering.

First, before hopping onto your bicycle and riding off into the sunset, check the tire pressure. Improper tire pressure causes more bicycle tire problems than any other factor—including dangerous blowouts. Don't judge by looking or feeling (the "squeeze" test just isn't very accurate). Use a tire pressure gauge—one designed to measure pressure up to and beyond the capacity of your tires (whether they be 50-, 70-, or 90-pound tires). If you regularly find one tire to be low, you should find the cause and correct it. It might be a slow leak from a small puncture or a defective air valve.

As you get started pedaling, apply the brakes to be sure they'll stop you properly. If you have gears, shift through them to see that they're all working.

As you ride along, listen to see if your bike has developed any strange new noises. If you'll be riding after dusk, make sure all lights are working and that your reflectors are in their proper place. All of these checks are designed to insure that you ride safely and to alert you to any changes that are occurring on the machine. Many times, the change can be corrected by one or more of the simple steps of TLC—Tightening, Lubrication, or Cleaning.

Tightening

Tightening and adjusting should be done periodically. It's a good idea to check every nut and bolt on your bicycle about once a month during the pedaling season. If you have a new bike right out of the showroom, even though it's been checked before it left the shop, you should check tightness after a week or so. Adjustments should be made on gears when needed. You should discover this need in your regular check each time you ride. If you have a bike without derailleur gears, you should check to see if the gear chain tension needs adjustment about once a month. Brake adjustment should also be included with your regular check before you ride, so you know if there's a problem developing before it becomes serious.

Regular lubrication of your bicycle helps minimize rust and only takes a few minutes a day. Many types of lubricants are now available.

Lubrication

Constant lubrication is necessary to keep your bicycle rolling along with a minimum of wear and rust. There are three basic types of lubrication used on a bicycle: oil, spray lube, and grease. The spray lubricants include WD-40, LPD, Handycan, and several similar products marketed by various bicycle manufacturers. These spray lubes are now applied to many parts that used to require oil.

There's a big advantage to using sprays. They dry clean and, therefore, don't attract dirt and dust the way oil does. With conventional oils, dirt accumulates quickly and the part can require much more frequent cleaning. These sprays also can be directed into tight places with greater accuracy than you could attain using an oil can. Use your favorite spray lube on cables, all pivot points for brake and gear levers, the chain, derailleurs, and the freewheel.

Monthly lubrication is sufficient under normal riding conditions. If your bike has been ridden in the rain, though, the use of a spray will help displace any trapped moisture. Some cyclists spray after each ride. This isn't really necessary, but it's quick and can do no harm. Pocket-size containers make it easy to carry spray lube with you at all times.

Oil can also be used on all these parts. There are several bicycle makers who put out their own brands of oil. SAE 30 is a good medium weight. Machine oil and gun oils are not as desirable, but it's better to use some sort of oil than to ignore all lubrication until you get the right kind. About the only place where oil takes precedence over a spray lube is where there are oiler caps on the hubs. These require about a teaspoon of oil each month. You should avoid using the lighter machine oils here, because they can dissolve the grease that has been packed around the bearings.

When oiling, be as neat as possible and don't allow oil to get on the tires. Oil will destroy the strength of the rubber in no time. Also, after you've finished, check a little while later to be sure there's no oil running down the spokes and onto the tires.

Grease is used primarily on bearings, and repacking is needed only after the bearings have been removed for inspection, and then either cleaned or replaced. Some hubs have grease fittings. These require a shot of grease every month or two. Use a light, low-temperature grease. Automotive grease that's made to withstand high temperatures is unnecessary. Lubriplate is good and is available at most bicycle shops and hardware stores. Many bicycle manufacturers also market their own brands of grease.

Cleaning

Bicycles should be cleaned regularly both inside and out. Some exterior cleaning should be considered after each ride. You should give your bicycle a quick visual check to see if you've picked up any road tar or mud. Also, inspect the tires to see if you've run over any oil spots on the road that may cause damage later. About twice a month, go over the entire bike with a damp cloth to remove dirt and dust. If there are stubborn spots, use a detergent or liquid cleaner. Road tar can be removed with kerosene.* The final step of exterior cleaning should include a good coat of clear wax on the frame and chrome. If you have been subjecting your bicycle to rough treatment, you may have to wax it every month or so. Under normal conditions, however, waxing is usually needed once or twice a year. Detailed instructions on caring for your bicycle's finish are included later in this chapter.

Inner cleaning of your bicycle consists mostly of inspecting and overhauling the bicycle's moving components. This includes the wheel hubs, headset, freewheels, pedals, bottom bracket, and derailleurs—if you have them. With all of these assemblies, you must disassemble, inspect, clean, regrease, and reinstall the part. For cleaning, you'll need to use some sort of solvent. Probably the least expensive (and fairly safe) is kerosene.* Never use gasoline, as it's very volatile. Even a spark can set it off. There are many other solvents for cleaning metal available at bike stores, hardware stores, and paint stores. Whatever solvent you choose, observe the cautionary instructions for your own safety.

In taking a unit apart for the first time, you should take careful note of where each part goes. You should also be aware that many ball bearings are not in a cage, but are merely loose inside. Be sure you don't lose any. If all the parts begin to confuse you, make a

---

*WARNING: When using a flammable liquid avoid inhaling fumes by providing adequate ventilation. Never work near a flame or spark-creating flame device.

diagram showing the sequence of disassembly. If there are loose ball bearings, count them to be sure you get the right number back in.

As you remove each part, put it in the solvent and let it soak. When you have finished the disassembly, carefully inspect each part. Look for such things as threads that are stripped, ball bearings that are pitted or worn, and bends in straight pieces of metal. The track or groove in which the ball bearings travel is called the race. Check this for pitting and wear. If any parts are damaged, replace them. Trying to "get by" with faulty parts can result in a major expenditure later on. If all of the parts are okay, take a discarded toothbrush and scrub them well. Dry them off by placing all the parts on an absorbent paper towel. When dry, you should pack the bearings in grease.

Cleaning and regreasing assemblies with bearings should normally be done about every six months. If for some reason you can't perform these simple care steps, take your bicycle into the shop and at least have the semi-annual cleaning and inspection of bearings made. At the same time, have everything else checked and adjusted.

Keeping Your Bicycle Fit

The following sections of this chapter will serve to acquaint you with most of the mechanical components and systems of your bicycle, as well as maintenance procedures to use. Some of them may require your attention only once or twice in the life of your bike. Others require continuous care and tuning if they are to perform at their peak.

Keeping your bicycle in top operating condition can be a source of great pleasure in itself. Bicycles are really simple machines compared, say, to a car. if you plan your maintenance operations before plunging into them, your bike will reward you with years of fine performance, and you'll derive a sense of personal satisfaction in knowing you're the principal reason.

The Steering System

The headset, the stem, and the handlebar comprise the steering system. A tourist handlebar with grips on the ends should have grips which fit snugly. If the grips are loose, replace them or try coating the bar end with rubber cement or contact cement. If after the cement has set overnight, the grip is still loose, buy new grips.

Drop or racing bars come in many shapes, some for road racing, track racing, or touring. These bars are usually taped. Use cotton adhesive-backed handlebar tape to obtain a sure grip on the bar. You can also use ¾-inch cotton twill tape (without adhesive), available at most dime stores. Actually, you can use almost any flat, fairly flexible, and relatively substantial material to wrap the handlebar; some people use the leather designed for wrapping the handle of a tennis racket. Rubber and plastic, however, don't provide as good a grip as cloth, especially when it gets wet or greasy.

Two layers of tape make for a thicker, more comfort-

The steering system consists of the headset, stem, and handlebar.

able grip. Many riders agree that adding this second layer eliminates hand discomfort. When the tape needs changing, of course, you need only change the top layer.

Drop bars should be angled properly. Even newly delivered bikes may have the bar set incorrectly. Most bars on touring and pleasure bicycles should be set with the lower hand-grip portion at an angle of about 10 degrees below horizontal. Change the bar angle by loosening the stem binder bolt, moving the handlebar and tightening the bolt again. When setting the bar, work from one side, using the bike's top tube as a horizontal reference point.

While handlebars and stems require no real maintenance, remember that when a handlebar or stem shows signs of cracking, it must be replaced as soon as possible, especially if it's made of aluminum alloy.

An aluminum bar that's been bent in an accident should be unbent very carefully or it may crack.

Never use a handlebar with an outside width greater than the outside width of your shoulders, as this is likely to cause fatigue. If your bar width is presently the same as your shoulder width, and you still fatigue too soon, try a narrower handlebar.

The stem bolt, which along with the specially shaped nut holds the stem into the steering tube of the fork, may have a hex-head top or an Allen-wrench slot. In either case, when removing the stem, unscrew the bolt slowly; it will seem to rise out of its hole. Tap it down gently with a soft-faced hammer or a regular metal hammer whose head is wrapped in cloth before it comes all the way out. This releases the truncated cone-shaped nut that wedges itself into the stem's slotted end and expands the stem. Now, remove the stem with a rocking motion.

When replacing the stem, put the bolt in its hole and screw the wedge nut hand tight, but not so tight that it spreads the slotted portion of the stem. Then insert the stem into the steering tube, rock it down into place—at least two inches into the tube—and tighten slowly. Don't overtighten. If your stem bolt has an Allen slot, use nothing but an Allen wrench or you'll risk stripping the slot, making it nearly impossible to remove the stem in the future.

Of all the bearings on the bicycle, the headset and its bearings require the least amount of attention. If the fork loosens—if it travels up and down in the head tube—mark the stem with a soft pencil so you know how deep it was in the steering tube. Loosen the stem bolt, loosen the top locknut with a wrench (but don't remove the nut), and adjust the top cup so that there's no longer any fork play. Then, slightly tighten the top locknut of the headset. Return the stem to its proper position, and finish tightening the locknut. If play still exists, start over.

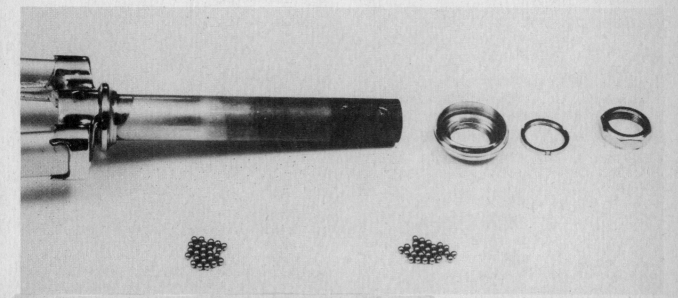

The headset consists of the fork, bearings, top cup, spacing washer, and locknut.

Use grease when overhauling, and don't attempt to lubricate between overhauls or you'll get lubricant on your front tire and brake pads. Do an overhaul every second season, whether or not you think it's needed.

Saddle And Saddle Post

Most of the rider's weight on a bicycle is supported by the saddle. People can sit on a badly adjusted seat for years and blame the seat for being uncomfortable. Generally, the flat portion of the seat, regardless of type, should be level. The usual reason for discomfort is that the nose of the saddle has slipped either up or down from true horizontal.

The seat post should be the exact size required for your particular seat tube. When reinserting a seat post in the tube, grease it lightly and wipe away the excess. The seat post should be inserted in the tube as far as it protrudes. If it is, it can't work its way out and damage the seat tube.

If your saddle is made of leather, treat it the way you would any other leather article. Clean it regularly with saddle soap and a good shoe polish, or use the expensive but excellent Proofide or Cadillac lotion. If you use shoe polish, use the neutral color, and rub it into the underside of the saddle, as well as on top. Use Neat's foot oil if you want to make the saddle more pliable, and a matching aniline spirit dye to hide scratches. Light coats of mineral oil or petroleum jelly are also good leather conditioners. To give the surface a shiny coat, use a spray lacquer or Neat-Lac, a lacquer-and-wax compound made especially for leather.

With leather or nylon racing-type saddles, the tension bolt should be fairly tight. The saddle should give a little, yet not be overly flexible. A good racing-type saddle should actually be more comfortable than a spring-type saddle, especially over long distances. Since the racing saddle is narrower, it should make less contact with the inside of your thighs, resulting in less chance for chafing.

The main cause of racing-saddle discomfort is overly tight tension and the nose of the saddle pointed up at too great an angle. Readjust the saddle whenever necessary, and you'll be surprised at the comfort it will give you.

Crank Components

The crank arms, chainwheels, pedals, and bottom bracket make up the crank system. Separate crank arms are either cottered—that is, a solid cotter pin holds the arm on the spindle ends—or cotterless, in which the crank arms bolt directly to the axle ends. Most cotterless cranks are made of high-grade aluminum, and most cottered cranks are constructed of steel.

To remove the cottered crank arms, use an adjustable wrench to remove the nut on the threaded end of the pin. Then place the hole in the handle end of the wrench over the unthreaded end of the pin. Using a C-clamp with a four-inch jaw, place the movable side over the wrench hole and the immovable side on the threaded end, and twist the clamp closed, squeezing the pin out. Hammering is taboo, since it will only deform the pin.

To replace cottered cranks, insert the pin in the crank arm, engaging the slot in the spindle. You can tap it lightly with a soft-faced hammer if it doesn't go in easily. Put the nut on the threaded end and tighten it firmly.

You'll need a crank remover to extract cotterless cranks. It's a bolt in the threaded bushing that threads into the dust cap threads in the crank arm. First, loosen the bolt and washer that push the arm onto the spindle, but don't remove them. Carefully thread in the remover bushing, and then slowly turn the remover counterclockwise. The remover bolt will bear against the concave head of the spindle-end bolt and push the arm right off. This job can be made easier with a long adjustable wrench.

The seat post should be the exact size required by the seat tube and the saddle should be level.

The crank system is composed of the crank arms, chainwheels, pedals, and bottom bracket.

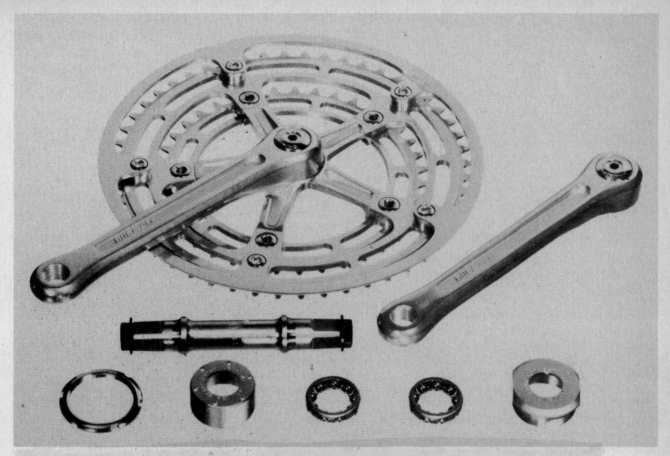

Better quality bikes usually have aluminum alloy cotterless cranks and chainwheels. Crank axle bearings are caged.

Be sure that the spindle ends and the corresponding crank-arm slots are clean when replacing the arms, and rub a film of grease on the spindle arm when you bolt the arms back on. For this, you'll need a crank installing tool or an appropriate socket wrench.

Be sure when examining the chainwheels that the wheels aren't bent, that the teeth aren't broken or badly worn, and that the bushings or bolts that hold them to the crank arms are tight. The chainwheel should be flat when dismounted from the assembly. If bent, it can be straightened in a vise off the bike. A minor bend or misalignment can be straightened with an adjustable wrench closed to the thickness of the chainwheel. Grasp the wheel with the wrench and pull it straight, but be careful of the teeth. If teeth are either broken or badly worn, replace the chainwheel. If your crankset is of an obscure brand, this is the time to replace it with a reputable brand that will fit.

To tighten or adjust the pedal cones, use a long-nosed pliers for grasping the flat sides of the cone. Pedals usually require several adjustments because it's hard to hold the cone in place while locking the locknut; so the cone often gets tightened with the locknut. You'll find it easier to tighten the locknut with an inexpensive open-end or box wrench of the appropriate size than with an adjustable wrench.

Pedals are designed to go on one side only. The right pedal is right-hand threaded and is marked with

A one piece cottered crank is usually found on less expensive bicycles. A cotterless crank is a good investment, as it will give your bicycle longer trouble-free wear.

When checking the chainwheels, look for worn or broken teeth, loose bolts, and bent wheels.

sions and riding over high curbs), almost nothing can go wrong with the frame. Even if you have minor falls or drive over bumps, not much is likely to happen to a properly constructed frame. Some mechanics can straighten a frame that has been bent; but if the tubes crack in bending, the frame is worthless and must be replaced. On more expensive frames, a tube can often be replaced, but this isn't a home remedy.

If your fork ends ever get bent out of parallel, you can straighten them. This can be done with a vise or with a long-handled wrench, both to the rear and front fork ends. Fork ends, even the best built ones, are quite flexible. You can bend them without fearing that they will break easily. Bent fork blades or steering columns can also be straightened; but we suggest you leave these jobs to professionals having the proper alignment tools.

an "R" at the threaded end of the spindle. The left pedal is marked "L," and is left-hand threaded; tighten it by turning counter-clockwise.

Bicycle Frame And Fork

The frame and front fork are the foundation of the bicycle. In normal riding (assuming you avoid colli-

Paint Care And Refinishing

Never allow the paint and chrome on your bike to deteriorate. Paint scratches and chips should be covered with touch-up paint, and the chrome should be polished occasionally with a chrome polish. Many bicycle dealers sell factory touch-up paint for better known bicycle makes. You can also protect the overall finish of your bike with a coat of clear lacquer or bicycle overcoat.

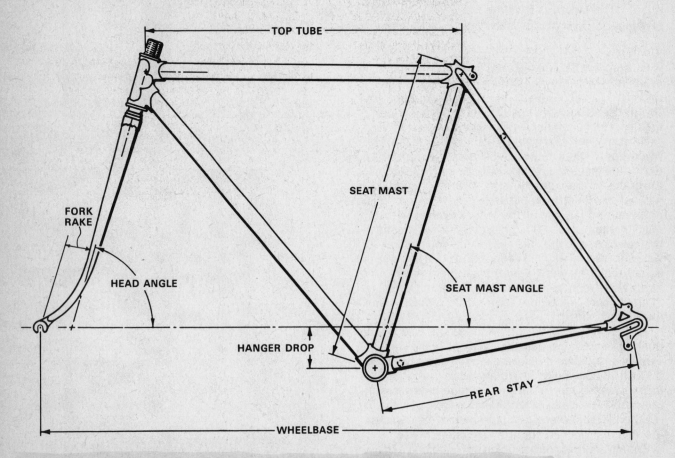

Since the frame and fork are the foundation of the bicycle, be alert for cracks and bendings of the tubes.

Whether the bike is lacquered or not, give it a wax coating with a clear liquid wax. Don't use the automobile waxes that dry to a cloudy appearance before you wipe them off; they'll only accumulate in the crevices and catch dirt. If you chip a decal or emblem, it can be fixed with touch-up paint.

You might want to repaint your bike's frame and fork. Use a good paint stripper and follow directions. (Be sure to wear rubber gloves.) Remove the finish down to bare metal, then sand and polish with 120-grit aluminum oxide cloth torn in ½-inch strips, using a back-and-forth motion. Wash the metal with alcohol or vinegar to remove all residues, then roll up newspaper and put a roll through the head tube and one through the bracket. These rolls should fit tightly to keep paint out. At this point, you have two options. Either prime and paint the frame yourself, or take it to a car painting shop and have them prime and paint the frame for you. They have a wide selection of colors, and they'll do an excellent job. You can usually get a finish as good as or better than the original, and it won't cost much.

If you decide to do the job yourself, prime the surface with zinc chromate primer, titanium dioxide, or aluminum primer and let it dry completely. Use spray cans in a well-ventilated, well-lighted area. If your bicycle has chromed parts, mask them carefully with masking tape and paper. Then use a spray enamel or epoxy enamel, applying two coats and letting the first coat dry overnight. Rub out bumps and runs after the first coat dries with #400 wet-dry sandpaper, and wash the dust away with alcohol before applying a second coat. The frame should be allowed to dry for a week (longer in damp weather) before reassembling the bicycle.

Whichever you do to your frame, refinishing it will be much cheaper than buying a new frame or a new vehicle, and the frame's new luster will give you miles of cycling pleasure over the coming years.

Fine-Tuning Adjustments

As you become more familiar with the workings of your bicycle, you'll probably want to perform more complicated adjustments yourself. Here are details on how to "fine-tune" three adjustable components—chains, gears, and brakes. The best guide for adjusting your particular kind of bicycle will be the owner's manual. These guides have a way of disappearing, though, so we've tried to include most of the different types.

Chain Adjustments

If your bicycle doesn't have derailleur type gears, the chain tension must be adjusted manually. At the center point between the front and rear sprockets, the chain should have about a ½-inch of play. A good way of checking this is to place a straightedge across the two sprockets. The amount of play will then be easy to see. If the chain needs adjustment, it's a simple job. Just loosen the mounting nuts that hold the back wheel either backward or forward to adjust the tension. When the tension is correct, retighten the nuts, making sure

that the back wheel is still properly aligned.

With a derailleur-equipped bicycle, chain tension is adjusted by the rear derailleur. If you have chain tension problems, you can take care of them when the derailleur adjustments are made. When replacing a chain, it's most important to get the correct length for your particular bicycle model.

Hub-Mounted Gear Adjustments

Gears and their shifting mechanisms for three- and five-speed bikes are located in the rear hub and stay in adjustment pretty well, but if they need any help, it's an easy task. There are three basic types of mechanisms. With all three, you should first put the shift lever into the middle gear. With the "Type A" mechanism, the gears are correctly adjusted when the adjuster rod is positioned so that it's exactly even with the end of the axle, as seen through the round access opening of the adjuster sleeve. To move the rod, loosen the locknut and twist the adjuster sleeve. When the adjustment is complete, tighten the locknut. This correctly adjusts all three gears.

The "Type B" shifter has an indicator rod located on the left side. The adjustment is made in the same manner employed with the "A" mechanism and is correct when the end of the rod is flush with the end of the axle.

Stem mounted gear shifters.

Down-tube mounted gear shifters.

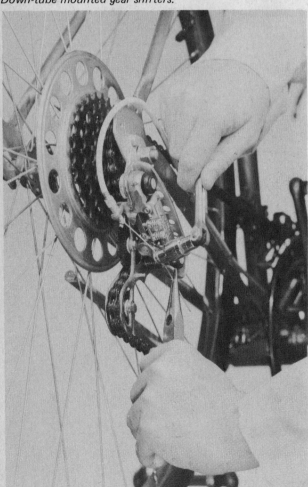

Cables must be pulled taut for derailleurs to function. For most rear derailleurs, the cable should be pulled taut with the chain on the smallest rear sprocket (high gear).

The "Type C" unit employs a right-side unit called a bell crank. It will have an arrow, line, or letter "N" that should be lined up in the center of a cutout.

The five-speed bicycle, with gears in the hub, will have two shift levers. The right lever will be adjusted by performing one of the above operations. The left-side lever will need only the proper cable adjustment. To test the cable, push the left lever back all the way. Push the arm on the bell crank forward as far as it will go. Now turn the rear wheel backward. If the turn of the wheel causes the arm to move forward a little more, you need to tighten the cable on the left side. It tightens by loosening the locknut and turning the adjusting sleeve.

Derailleur Gear Adjustments

Derailleur-gear shifters have all their components on the outside. Though they may look formidable, they're really quite simple to adjust.

A 10-speed derailleur system consists of levers (either handlebar-, stem-, or down-tube mounted), cables (which have different ball-ends than brake cables), front derailleur (steel or aluminum body, but almost always with a steel chain guide), and rear derailleur (steel or aluminum body with steel fittings).

Tighten the pivot bolt of the levers enough so that the cable tension doesn't pull the lever out of position. Conversely, if your bicycle often slips out of gear while rolling, the lever may be loose. Lubricate levers with a spray lube.

The cables must be pulled taut, with no slack, for the derailleurs to function. For most derailleurs, you must know the normal position of the component to make the proper adjustment. For most rear derailleurs, the normal position in which one should pull the cable taut is with the chain on the smallest rear sprocket (high gear). To adjust cable tautness on front derailleurs, you must determine if the cage rests low and is pulled up (from smaller to larger chainwheel) or vice-versa. Campagnolo front derailleurs rest low—Sun Tour Compe-V rest high. At any rate, pull the cable taut with the device in its resting position. The levers must be in the right position when you pull the cables taut. Handlebar levers must be all the way down; stem and down-tube levers must be all the way forward.

The main adjustments derailleurs need are setting the limit screws. These limit the side travel of both front and rear chain guides so that the chain can't be thrown off the gear sprockets. Determine which screw sets the limit for which direction, and set it so that the chain won't come off the gears, even if you pull the lever a little too hard. The only other adjustment you may want to make is to the front derailleur chain-guide cage.

The front derailleur unit will also have adjusting screws. However, some front units will have only one adjusting screw with the other adjustment being made by moving the chain guide in or out. Remember, the small front sprocket is low gear, and the large one is high gear—just the opposite of the rear unit. If your front derailleur has only one adjusting screw, the chain

When adjusting the low gear on the rear derailleur, the chain should be on the large sprocket.

High Gear Limit Screw

Low Gear Limit Screw

Cable Anchor Bolt

Chain Guide

The front derailleur is usually made of aluminum or steel with a steel chain guide. It has two shift limit screws.

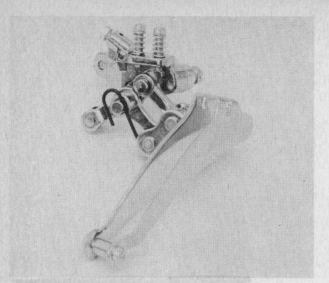

Adjusting a front derailleur involves tightening the limit screws.

guide is moved to adjust the low gear.

With the lever in low (small front sprocket), loosen the bolt that holds the chain guide and move it in or out until it's centered over the smallest sprocket. Before you tighten the bolt, be sure the slant of the guide parallels the surface of the sprocket. The lever is then shifted to high, and the adjusting screw is positioned to set the guide over the large sprocket. If there are two adjusting screws, you'll be able to see which is low by shifting into low and turning the screws to see which

moves the unit. Adjust low first and then adjust high. The guide should clear the sprockets by about ⅛ of an inch.

Brake Adjustments

The importance of stopping is obvious, and the wise cyclist knows that his brakes are among the most important mechanical features on his bicycle. There are two types of brakes on bicycles: coaster, or foot brakes, and caliper, or hand brakes.

Coaster brakes have all their parts in the rear hub. Fortunately, they rarely need adjustment. Repairing or adjusting these brakes requires expert attention because there are so many parts inside the hub. All the average cyclist need do is to be sure they're properly lubricated. When something goes wrong, you'll require factory instructions and an exploded drawing of the hub if you want to tackle it yourself. Until you have become very confident in your bicycle repairing abilities, this is a job best left to the qualified bicycle mechanic.

Caliper brakes are a different matter because all the parts are out in the open where they're easily seen and accessible. There are two types of caliper brakes: center-pull and side-pull brakes. Both are operated by squeezing a brake lever on the handlebar. The lever pulls a cable that pulls the brake unit closed, forcing two pads against the rims to stop the bike.

If the brakes aren't performing adequately, the first thing to check is the cable. If it has stretched, it may be too loose and needs to be pulled tight. At the brake

Rear coaster brake.

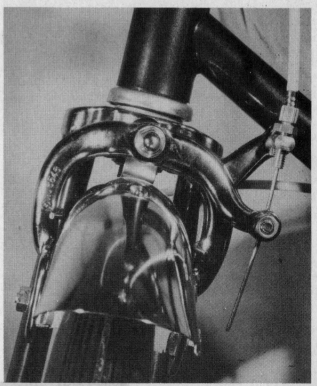

Side-pull caliper brake.

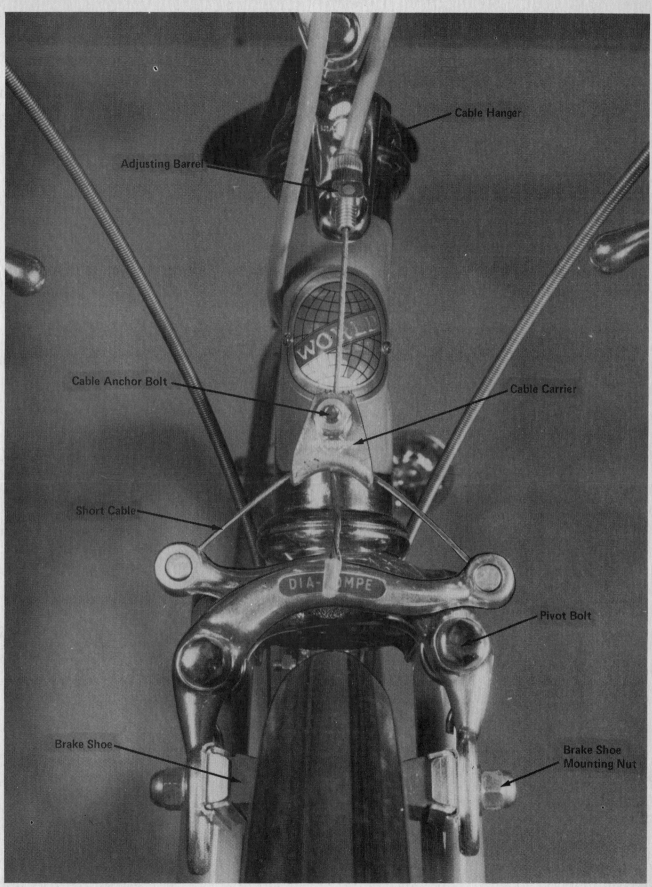

Cable Hanger

Adjusting Barrel

Cable Anchor Bolt

Cable Carrier

Short Cable

Pivot Bolt

Brake Shoe

Brake Shoe
Mounting Nut

Center-pull caliper brakes.

unit, there will be some sort of anchor bolt for the cable end. By grasping the end of the cable with pliers and loosening the anchor bolt, you can pull the cable tight. Also check the cable and its housing for kinks or frayed spots.

Next, check the brake levers to see that they compress and release easily. They require regular lubrication at the pivot points. The pads or brake shoes will gradually wear out. Inspect them and replace the rubber pads when they're badly worn or if the rubber has hardened. Since the pads must go against the rim of each wheel to stop the machine, inspect the rim surfaces. A bent rim, or one that has rough spots, won't allow the pads sufficient gripping surface. Also, look down at the wheel as it turns to be sure the alignment is straight. A wobbly wheel won't allow the pads to grip properly.

Next, look at the brakes while compressing the hand lever. If the pads strike part of the tire as well as the rim, they must be lowered. The brake shoes are positioned in a slot in the brake arm and held in place by an acorn nut. By loosening this nut, the pad can be adjusted up or down. Then, compress the hand lever and watch to see if both pads reach the rim at the same time. If not, the entire brake assembly needs re-centering. This is done easily enough by loosening the nut on the center bolt and moving the unit from side to side until it's centered.

You can adjust the shoes now. Measure the distance between the brake shoe and the rim. It should be about ⅛ of an inch. If it's not, loosen the adjusting nut and turn the adjusting barrel until the proper distance is attained. If the gap is so large that the adjusting barrel can't close it to the desired eighth of an inch, clamp the brakes against the rim and loosen the cable anchor bolt and pull the cable tighter. Then fine-tune with the adjusting barrel, as described above.

Buying Parts

If you live in or near a large urban area, you'll probably find several bike shops in your immediate vicinity. Most bike dealers who repair bicycles will have a supply of parts for many different brands and models of bicycles. Some will carry only parts for the makes they sell. After you have found out who stocks the parts you'll need, choose a dealer who seems to be most interested in helping you do a good job. Most will take the time to discuss your bicycle problems and answer any questions. Once you've found a repairman who is willing to help, go out of your way to help him in turn. Don't ask for detailed instructions on how to complete your do-it-yourself repair job when he's swamped with customers. Be sure all your friends trade with him, and that you buy all your parts, accessories, and future bikes from him. Make yourself known to be a good customer and the dealer will likely go out of his way to help you keep your bike in tune and rolling safely.

When you shop for a part, be certain that the part you buy is the correct one. If you have any doubts at all, take the old part in for comparison. If the exact replacement part isn't on hand, ask if there are interchangeable parts available from another manufacturer.

Bicycle Repairs

If you take proper care of your bicycle, you won't have many serious repairs to make. When your bike does need repairs, you may decide to take it in and let an expert do the necessary work. That's up to you, but there are some things you should know how to do, because you may need to make repairs when you're on the road with no expert bicycle mechanic around.

The Flat Tire

One of the most common problems you'll encounter is that old standby—the flat tire. A flat tire discovered in your garage is no problem. But one that occurs out in the country may leave you only one alternative to an on-the-spot repair—a long walk back to civilization. Obviously, if you're going to mend a flat, you'll need a spare tube, a spare tubular tire, or a patch kit. Even with the replacement for the flat, you must have an air pump to refill the tire. Some advance preparation, then, is certainly advisable before you begin any serious bike tripping.

The simplest and best insurance against the possibility of a flat is bringing along a spare. If you have sew-up tires, an entire new tire and tube will fit easily under your saddle or in some other out-of-the-way place. If you have clincher tires, you can carry a spare tube in the same manner. This way, the patching can be done at home at your leisure. Incidentally, your bike shop will carry a patch kit for your type of tire. However, if you have sew-up tires, the kit should include a needle, thread, thimble, and rim cement, in addition to the patches and patching cement. Such kits usually include detailed instructions with helpful illustrations.

For an air source, there are lightweight pumps that attach to the frame of your bike. Another item is necessary for foreign bikes whose valve stems are of the Presta or Woods type. It's an adapter that allows you to use compressed air from a service station in an emergency. (Some words of warning about service station air: add it in short bursts, only. It takes so little actual air to get a bike tire to the proper pressure that you may burst your tire if you're not careful. Also, some compressed air pumps deliver even short bursts of air with such power that they can overinflate one spot of a tube, causing a weak spot that sooner or later will explode.)

If you should have a flat tire, the first thing to check is the valve stem. Often, a leaky valve is the source of the problem. Partially inflate the tire and remove the valve cap. Place some saliva on your finger and rub it over the end of the valve. If a bubble appears, either tighten or replace the valve stem. This procedure is a lot easier than replacing the flat with your spare.

Since your patch kit will contain instructions on patching, only a few more precautions and tips are necessary. If you have clincher type tires (the kind with

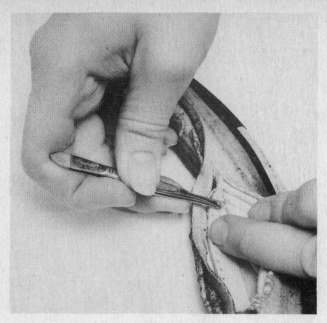

Tubular tires, with tubes sewn up inside, suffer more flats.

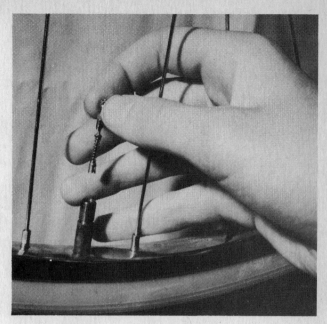

If you have a flat, the first thing to check is the valve stem.

separate tubes), try to remove the lip of the tire from the rim without using any kind of tool at all. Even special bike tire tools are liable to pinch the tube, resulting in problems later. Usually, you can roll the tire back with your hands, allowing you to get your fingers under its edge so you can pull the lip over the rim. Once you get part of the edge over the rim, the rest will almost be easy. Also, once you've patched a tube, inflate it and check for other leaks before putting it back on the bike. That could save you quite a bit of time and energy.

When you're ready to reinstall the tire on the rim, try to work it back in place without the tire irons, if possible. After installing either type of tire, inflate it only slightly at first to be sure the valve stem is coming through the rim straight and that nothing inside the tire is kinked. With sew-ups, check to make sure the treads are straight all the way around the wheel.

Cable Replacement

Every bicyclist should be able to replace the cables in the brake and gear systems of his bike. Even with proper care, these cables become frayed, wear out, and eventually break. A cable that has become frayed should always be replaced as soon as possible, or it's sure to fail when you're least prepared for it to happen.

It's important to remember that brake cables are a different size than derailleur cables. Cables for gears are a bit smaller in diameter. When replacing either type of cable, it's best to take the old cable to the shop to insure getting a cable that's long enough, has the proper tip on the lever end, and is of the proper diameter.

To replace a brake cable, you must first remove the old one. Loosen the anchor bolt at the brake unit. Then pull the cable out of the anchor. Next, squeeze the

hand lever, and the tip will be exposed. Take this end out of its slot in the handle and pull it to extract the entire cable. With the cable removed, inspect the housing to be sure it's still serviceable. Try to determine why the old cable wore out. You may have to correct something before you replace the old cable.

Installing the new cable should be easy. First, lightly lubricate it. Then, as you work it through the housing, starting at the lever, twist it against the way it's wound. This prevents the end of a strand from catching on something as it passes through the housing. When the cable has been anchored at the lever end, grab it with a pair of pliers to pull it tight. Make sure you have ad-

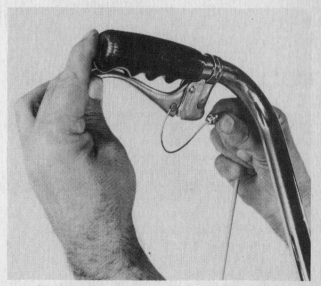

When installing the brake cable, make sure it is firmly attached to the lever.

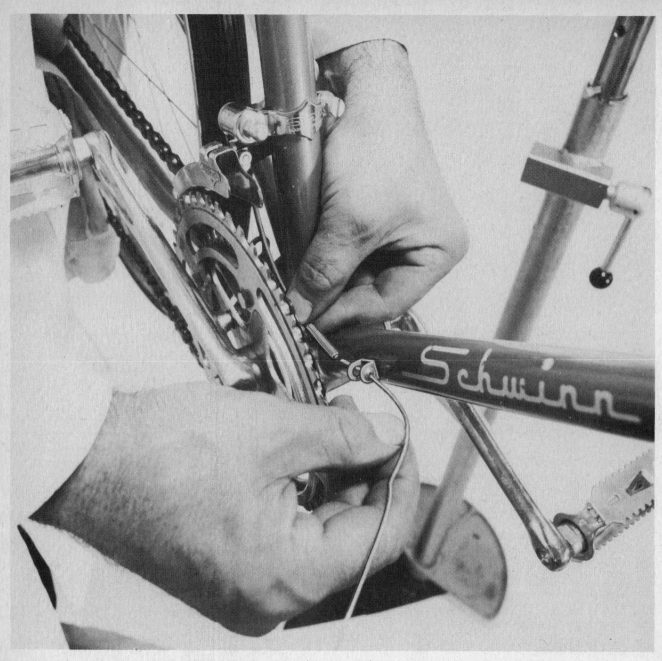

When changing a rear derailleur cable, the chain should be in the smallest sprocket. When reinstalling the cable, thread it through the stop and into its housing.

justed it so that the brakes work before you clip off what appears to be excess cable.

Derailleur gear cables are a little more complicated to remove. When removing a rear derailleur cable, have the chain on the smallest sprocket of the freewheel. Next, loosen the anchor nut at the derailleur. Move the hand lever as far in the opposite direction as possible. With most models, this will expose the cable end. Some levers will have to be taken apart to get at the end. Once you can get at the end, the cable can be pulled through and out.

With front derailleur cables, the same general procedure is followed. After you've anchored it in place,

shift from sprocket to sprocket to be sure it's properly connected.

With derailleur gears, never shift them without having the pedals turning. Here, again, don't clip off all the excess cable until you're sure it's adjusted properly.

Any new cable will generally stretch after use. Always check new cables for tightness after the first few rides.

Beyond The Basics

The care you give your bike will nearly assure its good health. However, things can go wrong, and we haven't

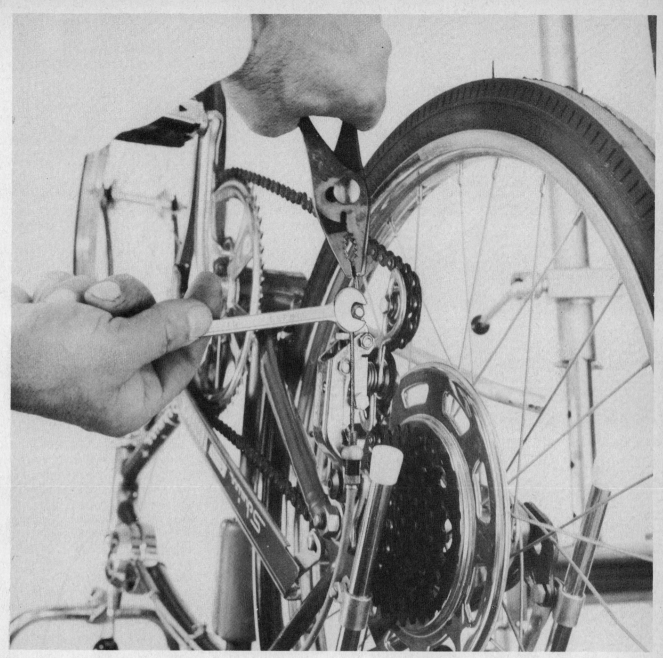

Once the derailleur cable is in place, pull the cable taut and tighten the anchor bolt. Don't clip off excess cable until you're sure it is adjusted properly.

mentioned how to overhaul your hubs or set your freewheel free. All of these things are within your capabilities if you want to do them. However, before you tackle any repairs that you're unsure of, seek out a good book that will explain in detail what's involved. Talk to other cyclists who may be able to give you the benefit of their personal experience.

Once you know what a certain operation entails, you may decide to ask a professional to do the job, or may decide to do it yourself. Probably the best way to prepare yourself for more involved repairs on your bike is to start off doing the easy things. As you gain confidence, you can attempt more complicated tasks.

Some of the jobs will be beyond your capabilities only because you don't have the tools or facilities to do them. In many cases, it would be economically impractical to buy some tools because you might use them only once or twice. Membership in a bicycling club may make it possible for you to have access to even the most exotic tools. If your club doesn't have a cooperative tool plan, mention it at its next meeting.

It's important to remember that many of the people who now make a living repairing bicycles were once as bewildered by these machines as you may feel today. But time has changed all that, as it may well for you, too.

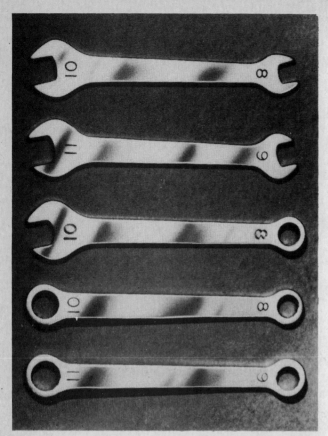

Assorted wrench set.

Bicycle tool kit.

Tools Of The Trade

To service your bicycle competently, you'll need several specialized tools, which you should be able to purchase from your bicycle dealer.

Spoke Wrench. This tool is used for tightening or loosening spoke nipples.

Wheel Hub Cone Wrenches. These are thin, strong wrenches for adjusting and removing wheel hub axle cone nuts and cone locknuts. You'll need two sizes—13-14 mm and 15-16 mm.

Freewheel Remover. This is a special tool to fit your particular freewheel. There are four different types of freewheels on the market, each requiring its own special tool. You'll need to remove the freewheel (on five- or 10-speed models) from time to time for cleaning and lubrication.

Crank Tools. On cotterless aluminum alloy cranksets, such as those made by Campagnolo, Stronglite T. A., and Sugino, you'll need a set of tools to remove and reinstall the cranks. These tools are necessary in order to be able to remove the cranks and get at the bottom bracket axle assembly for cleaning and periodic lubrication.

Bottom Bracket Tools. These are used to remove the bottom bracket cone and locknut, and include a special spanner to fit the locknut, and a special wrench to fit the cone. These tools vary in size depending on the make of crankset you have.

Chain Rivet Remover. This tool is used for five- and 10-speed chains. Other chains can be removed by prying off a master link with a screwdriver. But multi-speed chains are narrower, with little space between gears; therefore there's no room for a master link.

To remove a chain on a five- or 10-speed bicycle, the chain rivet removing tool is used to push a chain rivet out to where it's flush with the chain side plate. The tool is then removed and the chain twisted slightly at the loose rivet to make it come apart at that point.

To reinstall the chain, simply push the two ends together and with the rivet tool push the rivet back into place. Then twist the chain from side to side where the rivet was removed to take out any tightness at this point.

General Tools. These should include a set of metric socket wrenches from five to 22 mm, flathead and Phillips head screwdrivers in assorted sizes, and a small rubber-headed mallet.

Spring Service Checks

At least once each year, the following checkup should be given your bicycle—preferably before the peak bicycling season begins.

Tires. Inflate to full recommended pressure (check the side of the tires) and let sit overnight. Check the next morning to see if there are leaks.

Spokes. Go around the wheel to see that all spokes are tight and that they're evenly tensioned. If any spokes are missing, replace them.

Wheel Rims. Make sure the rims are true. Clean off

Five- and 10-speed bike chains require a chain rivet remover because of their narrow width.

drops of oil to the three-speed hub (an oiling hole is often provided).

Chain. Whether the bike is a coaster brake or multi-speed model, it's a good idea to remove, thoroughly clean and oil the chain before the start of every season. When installing the chain on three-speed and coaster brake bikes, leave ⅜ inch slack in the chain.

Crank and Front Sprocket. Check the condition of the grease on the crank bearings. If they're dirty and packed, cleaning and lubrication are in order. Check the cone adjustment—the crank should turn freely with no appreciable side-to-side play. With three-piece crank sets, check the tightness of all the mounting nuts and bolts, especially the crank-arm-to-spindle attachment.

Pedals. If the pedals don't turn easily or are worn or damaged, a new pair will improve cycling efficiency at a nominal cost.

Kickstand. Check the mounting of the stand to the bike. If it rattles or is loose, it should be repaired or replaced.

Derailleurs. If the bike is a five- or 10-speed model, clean off all accumulated road grit and grime from the derailleurs. Add one drop of oil at the pivot points.

Derailleur Controls and Cables. Clean any grime from the exposed sections of the derailleur cable, especially near the bottom bracket and rear stays of the bicycle. Lubricating the hidden sections of the cable with grease will make a world of difference in shifting ease. The grease will also help retard rust. Hook up the derailleur cables and check the operation of the derailleurs in all gears (while the pedals are moving—always).

Brakes. Clean all grit and grime from the brake assemblies and check the condition of the brake shoes. If the lugs or projections are almost worn off, replace the shoes.

Brake Controls and Cables. Make sure that each brake has a cable in good shape. Replace any cable that's badly frayed. Also watch for kinked or rusted cables and replace as necessary. Lubricating the enclosed sections of the brake cable will improve braking efficiency. Hook up brake cables and make sure that the brake shoes are evenly spaced from the rims. They should be about ⅛ to 1/16 of an inch from the rim.

Seat and Handlebars. Check to see that the adjustments are correct for proper fit and that all nuts and bolts are completely secured. Don't raise the saddle and seat post past the recommended heights. Remember that the seat and handlebar should be approximately the same height, and the seat should be horizontal (or close to it) and not excessively pointed down or up.

Paint Finish. Touch-up any nicks, dents, and scratches with touch-up paint. You can further protect a touched-up spot from rust by dabbing it with clear varnish. Use a clear, non-fogging type wax to protect the overall finish of the bike from the elements.

Follow the instructions with this annual Spring service check and you should be ready to enjoy a trouble-free riding season.

any accumulations of dirt and grime and remove whatever rust may be developing. If the bike is equipped with caliper brakes, make sure the rim is free of wax, oil, and other lubricants.

Front Hub. Make sure the axle nuts are securely tightened. If the front hub is equipped with a quick release mechanism, make sure the "adjusting nut" opposite the lever is set so that the lever holds the wheel securely. Check to see that the hub cones are properly adjusted. This can be determined by spinning the wheel. It should spin freely, but there should be no side-to-side play in the wheel. Check the lubrication of the front hub. If the grease is dirty or hard, clean and regrease the bearings.

Rear Hub. Check as you did the front hub. Also, check for lubrication and cone adjustment. If the rear hub is a three-speed unit, check the functioning of the hub in all gears. Make any adjustments as noted in your bike's owner's manual. Don't forget to add several

Bicycle Touring And Commuting

No one knows who the first bicycle tourer was. No one knows—exactly—what constitutes bicycle touring. Certainly an American by the name of Thomas Stevens was a bicycle tourer all the way back in 1884 when, urged on by fellow American cyclists, he became the first man to circumnavigate the globe on a two-wheeler.

In general, bicycle touring today means cycling for a fairly long distance. For you, that could be 10 miles. For an experienced tourer, it might be 75 miles or more—possibly even in one day.

Whatever distance one tours, one thing is certain. Touring is fast becoming a national mania. More and more Americans are finding the joys of hopping on a bicycle and setting off to see the country, whether on a half-day or a six-month tour.

Why all the interest in touring? Partly because man realizes he can move around freely without worrying about the high price or availability of gas. He doesn't need an expensive automobile. All he needs, in fact, are his own two legs and a cycling machine in reasonably good condition.

Where can one tour? Today, people frequently cycle all over the country. They explore the Rockies from Jackson, Wyoming, to Taos, New Mexico. They cycle along scenic Highway 1 overlooking the Pacific Ocean. They meander among the trees and wildlife in Yosemite. They marvel at the great north central flatlands of South Dakota and Minnesota, the waving fields of Kansas wheat, the hustle-and-bustle of Chicago. They cycle along the Mississippi River, retracing on land the path Mark Twain took so often via paddlewheeler. They even cross the Appalachians and travel up and down the Eastern Seaboard, from Florida to Maine—and beyond.

There's no end to where people can tour. Of course, not every minute of a bike tour is heavenly delight. There are hills to climb, rough roads (or no roads!) to traverse, harsh weather to endure. Yet the very obstacles encountered during a bike tour can add to the excitement and challenge of the trip. With a little knowledge and advance planning, you can overcome such difficulties and pedal on to new experiences. After all, isn't that what life is all about?

Touring Alone Or With Friends?

The pleasures of touring are enchanced when traveling with friends. Though there are advantages to solo cycling (you never have to wait for anyone and you can change plans as easily as socks), most riders agree that there's more fun in groups of congenial cyclers. Local bike clubs often sponsor such group trips, and there are a number of national organizations that can send you details about their bicycle programs. The American Youth Hostels, Inc. (National Campus, Deleplane, Virginia 22025), and the League of American Wheelmen (P.O. Box 988, Baltimore, Maryland 21203) are two excellent organizations. Contact them for information regarding organized bicycle touring.

When starting out, choose your cycling companions carefully. The friends with whom you tour should possess nearly the same ability. A strong cyclist feels frustrated pedaling the pace and distance of a bicycling tyro. The novice, in turn, may grow depressed in not being able to keep up with his faster-cycling friends.

Your cycling group should also be compatible in terms of activities and interests. Most importantly, ride with people who can face minor adversities with a smile; there are always some hardships along the way on any touring trip. You'll want to be with people who can laugh when things get rough.

If the group is small (three or four), you'll have few communication or logistical problems. Larger groups, however, demand some special precautions. Make sure that everyone knows the route, the stopping places, and the evening destination. In that way, not everyone will have to stay within earshot of the others. A successful tour should be flexible enough to allow for personal expression and experimentation, yet rigid enough so that no one ends up 50 miles behind the rest.

Some members of the group may want to do different things during the day, like stop at a nearby museum, go swimming in an inviting waterhole, or visit a local restaurant for lunch. If such activities mean the group won't be traveling the same roads, it's vital that each person know the way and the eventual meeting place to spend the night—or, on shorter tours, to begin the return journey.

If the members of the group are mature, road organization can be minimal. But young riders must be directed. The "locomotive and caboose" method is an excellent means for controlling the group without limiting the essential freedom of the riders. The locomotive is the person who leads the way, directing the group through confusing territory. No one gets in front of him; he knows the route and can read maps well. The caboose brings up the rear, carrying first-aid and bike-repair kits and having the knowledge to use them. No one gets behind him; he handles all the problems riders have along the way. The locomotive and caboose may be miles apart during a typical day on the road, but the group will all come together at the evening destination.

Planning A Tour

Bicycle touring is the least demanding form of travel in terms of advance planning. You can take potluck on meals and sightseeing during your tour, and you can take your choice of overnight accommodations from among camping sites, group hostels, and motels. Yet some planning must be done before you start pedaling. You must decide where you want to end up, how long you want to stay, and what sleeping arrangements suit you best. Then you must obtain the right equipment for your journey, and prepare yourself physically for your travels.

Most people are limited in the length of their tour by the length of their free time—whether weekend or vacation. In any case, one or two weeks is long enough for most but advanced tourers. Those lucky people with plenty of time on their hands must be careful not to

Touring takes you to many places that you'd never see in a car.

Solitary cycling can be as enjoyable as cycling with friends.

Roof-top bicycle racks enable you to transport your bicycle to whatever starting point you've chosen for your tour.

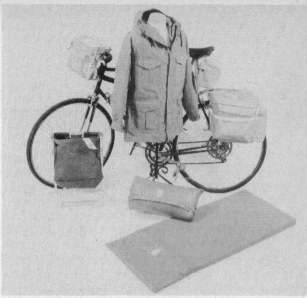

Packing light, but packing the right accessories, makes bicycle touring an easier, safer, and more enjoyable sport.

Bicycle camping trips are a great way to enjoy the outdoors.

plan an overly ambitious first effort. Only experienced bicycle tourists should consider even a month's trip or longer.

Some tourists transport their bikes to a jumping-off point, saving pedaling energy for scenic areas they'd like to explore far away from home. The simplest way to get your bike to the starting point is to carry it on a car bumper rack (a roof-top rack is the best way to transport a number of bicycles). If you plan to ship your bike by air or train, expect to remove the handlebar, turn the pedals inward, and place the cycle in a sturdy carton (often available from the transport company). Whenever shipping a bike, pad the derailleur carefully. If you ship it unboxed for some reason, be sure to remove accessories like pumps and water bottles, which have a way of getting lost.

Deciding where you want to go is strictly a personal judgement. Bicycle tourists travel just about anywhere—high mountain passes, deserts, and swamps—as well as beautiful countryside. Most people stick to paved roads for the majority of their trip, negotiating no more than a few miles of gravel when necessary. And many riders head for flat country rather than mountains for obvious reasons (though some hilly terrain is present on most every bike tour).

Your first job is to select a general region that you think you'd like to visit. The various sections of the U.S. offer diverse attractions (museums, sports, scenery, history, etc.) and you must decide what you want to see and do most. Of course, climate can also affect your choice. Springtime is rainy throughout the North and East, more pleasant in the South. Summer is fine most everywhere, though a bit hot in the South and Southwest. Fall is a generally nice season everywhere; but Winter means plenty of ice, snow, and "road closed" signs everywhere shy of the Southwest and Florida.

Give special thought to your evening arrangements. The youth hostel handbooks, campground directories, and motel listings can be quite helpful. Camping is the least expensive and the closest to nature, but it requires special equipment and expertise. To stay at a youth hostel, you'll need a valid hostel pass, a sheet sleeping sack, and the willingness to perform a few chores. If you elect to stay in motels or hotels, you can get by with the smallest amount of duffle. No matter what type of accommodations you desire, make the decision well before you're on the road.

Getting Outfitted

Though some die-hard cyclists have traversed the globe on three- and even one-speed bicycles, the modern 10-speed derailleur-equipped bike now dominates the touring scene. It's efficient, making long-distance pedaling a joy rather than a drudgery. If your 10-speed bicycle isn't something special to you when you begin a tour, it almost certainly will be after you've pedaled perhaps hundreds of miles on its 25 pounds of metal tubing and rubber. A bike for touring should be as light and as well constructed as you can afford. It must be strong enough to absorb the punishment of rough

roads even when fully loaded. If you learn to ride it well and keep it in fine tune, you'll enjoy touring to the fullest—and you'll want to go out again trip after trip after trip.

Since the most common ailment in touring is the flat tire, carry a tube patching kit. (Be sure the rubber cement hasn't dried with age.) Have tire irons along to get the tire off the rim, if necessary. If you use a screwdriver, you'll wind up with more punctures than when you started. Thorn-resistant tubes all but eliminate punctures, but they're much heavier than standard tubes. No matter which tube type you choose, always start a long tour with new tires and tubes and carry a spare tube for emergencies.

Take the tools that came with your bike or carry a 6-inch adjustable end wrench. A small screwdriver and a chain tool are other necessities. With a chain tool and a few extra links, you can repair a broken chain in minutes. On longer tours, carry some extra nuts and bolts, a section of brake cable (long enough to fit the rear brake), some brake blocks, and lubricating oil.

The clothes you wear on tour are determined by the climate in which you cycle. Double knit and permanent press fabrics are excellent; socks and underclothing should be of a quick-drying type. If you coordinate your colors, you'll be able to mix-and-match your outfits. For warm weather, shorts and cycling jerseys (or short-

A first-aid kit is a must on any bike tour.

sleeved knit tops) are ideal for men and women. During cooler spells—or for evenings—warmer clothes such as knickers or jeans with a long-sleeved shirt or sweater are good.

Shoes are so heavy that you should take only one or two pairs. One pair should be suitable for cycling and walking, the other for dress (if necessary). A wind-breaker jacket for cool mornings and chilly evenings, swim clothes, pajamas, cycling gloves, a brimmed hat to keep the sun out of your eyes, and perhaps a sweater complete the typical wardrobe.

Pedaling in the rain demands some special gear like two-piece rain suits. Many rain suits can be folded and carried in a waistband pocket. Suits made of urethane-coated nylon are completely waterproof and light-weight; but since they don't breathe, condensation of body perspiration can leave you drenched. Recently, 100 percent waterproof rain gear which eliminates the condensation problem—made of "no-sweat" knit fabric—has been imported to America. This rainwear allows water vapor to be dispelled while keeping out the foulest weather.

Packing Up

Once you assemble all the gear you're taking on tour, you must find a way to load it on your bicycle so that it will ride well throughout the tour. Proper packing takes practice. Veteran tourists pack their saddlebags to show the top of each item. Using this vertical packing system, they need only lift the saddlebag flap to see everything. Moreover, grouping items together—in plastic bags for extra protection—helps keep them

orderly. For example, you should keep all of your sleeping gear together. Otherwise, you'll have to unpack all your sacks to get the items you'll need for bedtime.

The key to successful packing for a bicycle tour is starting early. Assemble all your equipment with time enough to try several different loading systems until you find the best one for you. It should be an enjoyable project unless you put it off until the last possible minute, when your mood may be anything but pleasant.

Load your gear and take a shakedown cruise at least a day before you start touring. Pedaling a few miles around the neighborhood will tell you whether you should rearrange some of your duffle. Next, head for the back yard and set up your camping gear, if you'll be tenting or sleeping under the stars in a sleeping bag. Go so far as to prepare a meal on your backpacking stove—just to be sure everything is functioning well and you haven't forgotten how to use it. The practice you get setting up and striking camp will save you from looking like an amateur on your trip.

If you plan on touring tandem, be aware that there are fewer places to pack things than there are on two single bicycles. Tandem touring is great fun, but it calls for special planning.

Physical Preparation

All tourists begin their trips with plenty of enthusiasm, but only the best conditioned are still smiling a few miles down the road. Bike touring isn't a demanding sport; but it does require some physical preparation.

The best physical exercise in preparing for a tour is

Tandem touring is a popular new sport.

touring—or mock touring. Find out in advance how far you'll be pedaling on an average day and gradually work-up to that distance over a few weeks' time. Constant riding will get your legs and lungs in top shape. But there are other benefits, as well—especially for the beginning tourist. Riding every day is the best way to break-in a new saddle, familiarize yourself with your bike, make minor fitting adjustments, and practice bicycle maintenance procedures.

Touring Tips

One of the best tricks to making bicycle touring an enjoyable experience is to get an early start each day. Although getting up early may not be your particular idea of a good time, the alternative is to find yourself hurrying along during the hottest part of the afternoon in order to reach your destination. It's much better to get up a bit earlier, have a simple breakfast, and get in two-thirds of your biking before lunch. Then you can eat a leisurely meal, rest, see a few sights, and still pedal to your stopping place with plenty of time to shower or take a quick swim before dinner.

Try to arrive at your campsite with at least two hours of daylight remaining in order to set up your camp. Since most hostels open in the late afternoon, plan to arrive there—unless you have reservations—between 4 and 5 p.m. If you have reservations, you can arrive a bit later, but allow yourself enough time to check in and cook dinner. You can arrive at a motel most anytime as long as there's a vacancy. (Reservations are a good idea).

Many bike tourists find that a noontime picnic can be one of the most enjoyable periods of the day. The backdrop for your lunch may be a mountain range, forest, or broad, winding river. A few items of equipment will make your lunches go more smoothly. A square of plastic on which to lay food, a personal cup in which to mix fruit drinks and powdered juice, a pocket knife for slicing and opening, and a salt shaker will come in handy.

The lunch, itself, may vary from sandwiches and cookies to fruit, cheese, hard-boiled eggs, carrot and celery sticks, potato or corn chips, and a host of other edible goodies. Be sure to sample the local specialties when pedaling through an area.

Most bikers like to snack during rides. A wide range of suitable items are available from the supermarket, sporting goods stores, and health-food stores. Some of the choices are fresh and dried fruits, nuts, cookies, fruitcake, honey combs, crackers, pretzels, and beef jerky. In addition, riders must always carry their own water bottle. Your body is your power source when you're on tour, and it doesn't work well when you're hungry or thirsty. So eat and drink often, and keep your energy coming in abundant supply.

Bicycle Commuting

As the cost of driving to work continues to climb, more and more urbanites are discovering the value of bicy-

Plenty of leisure time for sightseeing adds fun to any bike tour.

cle commuting. In general, much of what we've said about bike touring can be applied to bike commuting—with the exception, of course, of sleeping overnight.

Before you undertake commuting to and from work by bicycle, make sure your machine is in peak operating condition. There's nothing worse than having a breakdown on you way to work. Not only do you run the risk of arriving late, but changing flats and making repairs en route can leave you dirty, tired, and frustrated before your "real day" begins.

The key to successful bicycle commuting is to allow yourself plenty of time. To find out just how much time is required, take a trial trip from home to office on a weekend and then double that time to allow for increased traffic and other problems in weekday commuting. A nice, leisurely bicycle trip to and from work can do wonders for your mental attitude—as well as your physical conditioning. Forcing yourself to complete X number of miles in a limited amount of time, however, can add to overall frustrations and poor frame of mind.

When commuting by bicycle, be sure you have the same tools you'd take on a bicycle tour. In addition, you should equip your bike with whatever accessories you might find convenient. These probably will include a good pair of saddlebags and spring-loaded carrier in which you can bring such items as sportcoat and tie (if required in your job), dress shoes, briefcase, and books. Also, be sure that, once you arrive at your destination, there's a safe, convenient place to lock your bike. As bicycling's popularity continues to grow, so, too, do bicycle thefts. Lock your bike for the day with a sturdy cable-type "chain" and a large, sturdy key-type lock. Or, better still, bring your bicycle right inside the building whenever possible. You might check with the building maintenance person to see if there's storage space in a little-used corridor or the boiler room.

Safe Cycling

Bicycling is a healthy, enjoyable activity currently pursued by 100 million Americans—nearly one out of every two men, women, and children living in the U.S. It's as close to the ideal pastime as one can get—or, at least, it would be except for one thing. Each time a bicyclist mounts-up for a leisurely jaunt around the block or an extended tour across country, he risks his safety—sometimes even his life.

The average bicyclist today has about two chances in five of experiencing an accident which results in physical injury or property damage. He has approximately one chance in 25 that he'll require medical treatment. Though the chances that a cyclist will collide with an automobile—the ultimate risk in bicycling—are less than one in 200, these odds were enough to result in nearly 1,000 deaths and 60,000 injuries in 1978.

If these figures sound alarming, let's look at them another way. Your chances of colliding with an auto are less than .5 percent if you're an average cyclist. If you are above average in your concern for bicycle safety and always cycle cautiously, the percentage risk that you'll be in an auto-bike collision is even lower. On the other hand, if you completely ignore the basic rules of safe cycling, your chances of having a serious collision greatly increase. The choice is up to you.

New Safety Regulations

Safe cycling starts with a safe bicycle. Seventeen percent of all bicycle-related injuries result directly from mechanical or structural failure. Reacting to these statistics, the Consumer Product Safety Commission has set certain bicycle standards (which became effective May 11, 1976) for all bicycles sold in interstate commerce (except for racing or custom-built bicycles). These standards delineate minimum and maximum limits for a bicycle's structural strength, design, and ease of assembly. Some of the rules include the following:

Brakes. To meet the requirements, a bicycle with hand brakes (which comprise the great majority of adult bicycles sold in the U.S.) must be able to stop within 15 feet after reaching a test speed of 15 miles per hour. The maximum dimensions of the brake lever from the outside edge of the handlebar must not exceed 3½ inches. The brake pads have to be adjustable and replaceable and cannot contact the tires or spokes. Additionally, the brake shoes can't slide out of their holders when the brakes are applied and the bicycle is rocked back and forth.

Similar standards are specified for coaster-brake bicycles with the additional specification that the crank won't have to be turned more than 60 degrees before the brakes are applied. Sidewalk bicycles with a seat height of less than 22 inches have to be equipped with a coaster brake that meets all standards set for coaster-brake bikes or there has to be a clearly visible marking on the bicycle that says, "No brakes."

Steering. The handlebar stem must have a mark indicating the minimum length that the stem has to be placed in the frame. The ends of the handlebars have to be at least 14 inches, but not more than 28 inches apart, and the ends must be plugged with either grips, plugs, or shifting devices. Finally, if the bicycle is sold unassembled, the consumer has to be clearly warned of the danger of overtightening the stem bolt (overtightening this bolt could weaken the handlebar stem and cause it to fail).

Protective Guards. Bicycles with a single front and single rear sprocket must be equipped with a chain guard which covers the chain from 3.2 inches from the rear hub up to and 90 degrees around the front sprocket. A test is also specified which is intended to prevent a finger from becoming caught between the front sprocket and the chain. Derailleurs must be guarded against either stopping or interfering with the rotation of the wheel. This would seem to mean that all derailleur bicycles should be equipped with a rear spoke protector.

Tires. Tire inflation pressure must be clearly stated on the side of the tire (except for sew-ups and semi-pneumatic tires). Wheels must be secured to the bicycle with some sort of positive locking device. Quick-release hubs must be adjustable for tightness and indicate whether they are in the open or locked position. The clamping action of the QR lever has to be strong enough to leave "bite" marks in the fork.

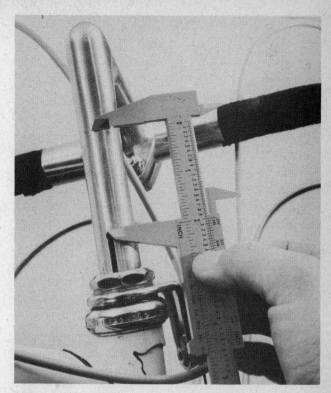

Make sure the handlebar stem is placed correctly in the frame.

Reflectors. Every bicycle must be equipped with a clear front reflector, amber or clear pedal reflectors on both sides of the pedals, and a red rear-facing reflector. Side reflectors may be either spoke-mounted reflectors or reflectorized tires. The reflectors have to pass rigid photometric tests and must be protected from hitting the ground even when the bicycle is allowed to fall.

Reflectors are an important part of safe cycling.

Have a friend help check your bicycle for safety.

Other. Every new bicycle must be accompanied by an owner's manual and, if the bicycle is less than completely assembled (like Huffy, AMF, Murray, etc.), there must be a complete and clear set of assembly instructions included. Bicycles must also be labeled with the statement, "Meets U.S. Consumer Product Safety Commission Regulations for Bicycles." All cycles must be permanently marked with the name of the manufacturer or private labeler and there must be some sort of date code by which the month and year of manufacture can be determined.

Checking For Safety

When you're buying a new bicycle, check for cracks (rare—but they do occur) in the frame or fork assembly. Also watch out for bends which may have occurred in shipping. Check for broken spokes, wheels that wobble or don't spin freely, and non-functional brakes.

You should inspect your own bicycle periodically for these same flaws. Tire pressure should be checked and the recommended pressure maintained. Underinflated tires can make your riding unstable and fatigue you unnecessarily, but overinflation can reduce traction and increase the possibility of a blowout. Pedals should be kept in good condition and, when needed, be replaced with non-slip reflectorized pedals. Any reflectors on the bicycle should be kept clean, and lights should be working and visible at least 500 feet in front and 300 feet to the rear.

The front wheel is held in place by the front wheel nuts, which should be kept tight and checked as a matter of habit. Many accidents are caused by pant-legs or toes which become trapped in the front sprocket. Either wear tight-fitting pants or a pant guard and shoes whenever cycling, and keep the chain or derailleur guard in place for extra insurance. A loose seat is a hazard that can send you sprawling, so keep it tight enough to prevent it from rotating or sliding.

Finally, if your bicycle is equipped with hand brakes,

the pivot points on the calipers should be kept well oiled, and binding brake cables should be replaced. Be careful not to get oil on brake pads or wheel rims, as this will make your brakes ineffective.

A Perfect Match

A bicycle should fit the rider and his capabilities for safe, happy cycling. A Canadian study found that a youngster increases his chances of having an accident which involves personal injury by five times when riding a bike that's too large and by three times when riding a bike that's too small. This emphasizes the fact that a bicycle should be fitted to the present size of the rider and not purchased with the idea that the rider will "grow into" it.

A correctly sized bicycle will allow the rider to straddle the top bar of a man's-style bike while standing flatfooted, with about one inch of clearance between the rider and the bar. When seated, with one foot on a pedal in the "up" position, the ball of the other foot should reach the ground when the bicycle is tilted just slightly to that side.

A bicycle should also fit its rider's characteristics. There's no one design that's best for everyone, but there is a design that meets each person's individual needs. For example, front and rear caliper brakes, properly applied, can stop a bicycle traveling at 15 miles per hour in a five to 10-foot shorter distance than can coaster brakes. But an inexperienced, weak, or uncoordinated person may not be able to stop at all by using hand brakes—or worse, he may grip the front brake too hard and be pitched over the top of the bike. As a result, young children should be wary of caliper brake bikes. They should ride bicycles equipped with standard coaster brakes until they're old enough to know how to use caliper brake models, and be physically able to use them.

The same principle applies to the type of gearing selected on the bike. For the young child or novice rider, a derailleur gear mechanism is too complex to use and may demand the rider's full attention when he should be watching for traffic. A tangled chain or slipping pedal due to misuse of derailleur gears has caused many accidents and injuries.

Likewise, rattraps (those cage-like devices into which the tips of the toes slip for improved pedaling efficiency) are a real detriment to youngsters and to many older persons, as well. It's difficult for many people to slip into the traps without looking down at the pedals, which could cause an unexpected veer into traffic.

Like an automobile, the sportier the design of the bicycle, the more skill that's often required to operate it safely. Consider this when looking at the popular hi-rise and racing-style bicycles around today.

The safety of the hi-rise bicycle has been the topic of many discussions and arguments in recent years. A National Safety Council survey showed that in 1972, two-thirds of the bikes ridden by school-age children were of the hi-rise type (with exceptionally high handlebars). This survey showed that the number of accidents per mile ridden was actually lower for hi-rise bikes than for standard bicycles. This doesn't prove that hi-rise bicycles are safer, however. Additional studies have shown that hi-rise bicycles produce 12 percent more head injuries and that they tempt youngsters to ride "double" or even "triple" and to attempt to perform various unsafe stunts while riding. There seems to be little doubt among serious cyclists that hi-rise bikes are more difficult to control under less-than-perfect road conditions than standard machines.

Here are some current thoughts regarding hi-rise bicycles and their purchase and use.

1. A beginning cyclist should learn to ride on the more stable, conventional bicycle with its even weight distribution, longer wheelbase, and high wheels.

2. Bicycles with excessively small front wheels can easily flip over if they hit a hole or curb.

3. Hi-rise bicycles with a "stickshift" or anything sticking up from the top frame bar can cause serious injuries and probably do not meet safety regulations.

4. Hi-rise handlebars should not be angled back towards the body of the rider to compensate for size, as this can interfere with turning. Handgrips should never be above shoulder height.

The lightweight racing-style bicycle, while not as radical a design as the hi-rise machine, should also be considered carefully before purchase. While ideally suited for long-distance riding at relatively high speeds, the low angled forward posture demanded by the handlebar configuration in drop-bar bikes makes it harder to see and be seen in traffic. Also, the complex gearing system can jam and leave the inexperienced cyclist vulnerable in the midst of an intersection. For stop-and-start city riding, a more conventional bicycle might be a safer choice.

Skillful Cycling

The first step towards bicycle safety is learning how to ride skillfully and maintaining complete control of the bicycle at all times.

Nearly ten percent of the people responding to a National Safety Council bicycle survey stated that they fell down the last time they rode prior to the survey. Ten percent!

For those who are just learning to ride, falling is a common event. That's why a person should learn to ride away from traffic, in an empty parking lot or on a dry, grassy surface away from any obstructions (like mailboxes, lamp posts, and fire hydrants). The best bicycle to use is one that's just a little too small and has a "girl's" frame. Methods vary, but it's a good idea to learn the use of brakes early in the lesson.

The more experienced rider can practice and improve his riding skills by trying these exercises in an empty parking lot or on a school playground.

Balance. From a standstill, ride slowly between two straight lines two feet apart and 75 feet long without touching either line.

Maneuvering. Set up a line of empty milk cartons 6

The safety of hi-rise handlebars has been the topic of many discussions. Any child first learning to ride a bike should not be taught on a bicycle with a hi-rise style handlebar.

to 8 feet apart. Start back 20 feet, then zig-zag to the right of the first carton, to the left of the second, and so on, slalom-style. If that seems too easy, move the cartons closer together.

Stopping. Have a friend help with this exercise, which entails riding in a circle around him. When he yells, "Stop!" see how far it takes you to come to a complete stop.

If you ride a bicycle with a derailleur, practice changing gears smoothly and accurately away from traffic while keeping your eyes on the road. Never change gears while pedaling hard. Besides damaging the gears, the chain may slip and throw you off balance. When coming to a stop from high gear, always downshift to a lower gear before stopping. This will allow you to accelerate rapidly with the least amount of wobble. This is an important ability when crossing intersections, for example.

There's more to safe riding than skill and control. Knowledge and wise use of the rules of the road and driving conventions are essential to the prevention and avoidance of accidents. Because most children learn to ride a bicycle by the age of five, parents have the primary responsibility for teaching them basic safety rules.

For those learning to ride in traffic, riding and safety information are available from the American Automobile Association and the National Bicycle Dealers Association. Many local police departments and schools have organized bicycle safety instruction; and an excellent curriculum entitled, "All About Bikes," is available from the National Safety Council.

You should remember when cycling that a bicycle

Obeying the rules of the road means not riding double.

Cyclists must obey traffic laws like any other driver.

ridden on any road is a vehicle, and it has the rights and restrictions defined by vehicular laws. This means that the bicyclist must obey such regulations as riding on the right-hand side with the flow of traffic and obeying all traffic signs and signals.

The lack of uniform traffic laws in the U.S. is one problem that should be corrected at the Federal level. Laws generally prohibit riding double on a bicycle not designed for two, riding at night without a light, and hitching rides by holding onto a moving vehicle. The laws should also restrict bicycle riding to the right-hand side of the street and require the use of a bicycle path, if present.

In most states, hand signals are required before a turn, but the method of turning isn't always prescribed. There are, though, correct ways of turning which should be followed for safety's sake. Right turns are relatively simple. Signal well ahead of time, or when stopped at a sign or signal. Keep right at all times and don't swerve left into traffic.

Left turns may be made in one of two ways. The right-angle method is the safest and should always be used at night. It's also best in heavy traffic and at multi-lane intersections. As you approach the intersection, keep right, near the curb, and—when safe— proceed across the roadway. Then, when the way is clear, turn in your new direction and continue.

The other method is to signal left before the intersection and switch to the left side of the lane. Remain near the center of the road until the way is clear and then turn left. This method is potentially dangerous, though, and should be used only on streets with light traffic and good visibility. Remember, in a hazardous situation, you can always dismount and walk your bicycle. As a pedestrian, you have the right of way.

Defensive Cycling

There are many other safe cycling tips which are not laws, but should be remembered. Before taking a ride, you should be sure any packages you're carrying are packed securely in a basket or carrier. Weight should be distributed evenly from side to side, and front baskets or carriers shouldn't be overloaded.

Obey all of the rules of the road and beware of typical driving hazards, but also beware of specific hazards which plague cyclists in particular. Watch for sewer gratings which may trap bicycle wheels. Bumps, potholes, mud, loose gravel, and leaves (especially when wet) can cause a sudden spill. Bicyclists must also be especially careful when avoiding these problems because car drivers behind won't be looking for sudden swerves or stops. Rain affects autos and bicycles alike because the roads become slippery and visibility is reduced. Cyclists with handbrakes should be very careful because water on the wheel rims or brake pads can more than double the required stopping distance. One remedy for this is to ride a short way with the brakes applied lightly until the rims and pads have dried somewhat, after which time normal braking power will be regained.

The use of hand signals is another area where intelligence, as well as knowledge of the rules of the road, is required. By law, signals are required before any turn or stop. A left turn is signaled by extending the left hand straight out, away from the side. For a right turn, the left arm is bent up at the elbow; it's bent downward from the elbow for a stop. On most hand-brake model bicycles, the rear brake lever is on the right, so one-handed braking is possible while signaling without losing control of the cycle.

A bicycle requires both hands for full control, so, in a tight situation, the cyclist is forced to choose between signaling and maintaining control. Naturally, it's best to do the latter. This contradiction has caused some experts to question the value of hand signals altogether. Nevertheless, signals shouldn't be abandoned, for they're a valuable means of telling other vehicles what you intend to do. No one, of course, would suggest that you signal if there's the risk of losing control, but the safe cyclist shouldn't have to make this compromise. He should signal well ahead of a turn or stop and should avoid hazardous situations by slowing down and, when necessary, dismounting and walking the bicycle.

The urban cyclist should also be wary when riding alongside of parked cars. A suddenly opened door or a car pulling out of a driveway can cause serious damage and injury. As a defensive rider, you should be constantly alert for evidence that a door is about to open or that a car is about to pull out. For example, watch for exhaust fumes, the sound of an engine, or the sight of a driver in a parked car. Slow down, use a bell or horn to signal your presence, and—most of all—be alert.

Dogs can also create unexpected problems for the cyclist. There's something about a bicyclist that seems to grate on the nerves of even the most even-tempered canine. Most animals are content to run alongside a cyclist and bark; these can be ignored. A particularly persistent dog can be discouraged by dog repellent spray, which should be a staple for any bike tourer or commuter. You should resort to special measures only if there's no traffic and if you're in complete control of your bicycle. Never kick at a barking dog, however, as you'll probably just incense the animal and may even lose control.

The best way to avoid occasional hazards is to plan your route before you ride. If possible, route your ride around that pesky dog, the rows of parked cars, and that left turn at a busy intersection. If you're fortunate enough to have bicycle paths nearby—or even marked bicycle routes—use them whenever possible. If you're planning to use one particular route for commuting, ride it first on a weekend and make note of potholes, blind spots, and dangerous intersections. Try to plan your trips for times when traffic is light, and avoid "through" streets, especially if the speed limit is more than 35 miles per hour.

When planning a ride through a rural area, don't relax your safety standards. Nearly half of all bicycle fatalities occur in rural areas on open highways. The high speeds encountered there require you to be constantly alert and on the defensive. A car going 55 miles per hour travels the length of a football field in 1.2 seconds. You must stay out of its way because it won't be able to get out of yours.

No More Second-Rate Citizens

The Federal Highway Act of 1973 heralded a new era for bicycles. It struck a blow against the philosophy that

Bicycles should be walked across hazardous intersections.

cars have priority to roadway space. Bicycles were recognized as legitimate users of the nation's streets. City planners can't design roads for motor traffic and sidewalks for pedestrians, and then leave tens of millions of cyclists to fend for themselves. Recently, hundreds of bills have made their way through various state legislatures for the design, construction, and maintenance of bike paths. Bicyclists are no longer second-rate citizens!

The steadily increasing number of cyclists and the rising number of bicycle-auto collisions have indicated the necessity for these bikeways. Washington, D.C., like many other large cities, has reported 6,000 bike commuters in good weather. New York City has more than 10,000 bicyclists in the city park system on a sunny day. Several transportation contests in Atlanta and Boston have revealed that the bicycle can often be faster than other modes of travel during rush-hour trips of about five miles in length, to say nothing of offering fewer parking problems! The environmental pollution problems and now the energy shortage with rising gas prices have further turned the legislators' attentions to bicycle pathways.

The popularity of bicycling is resulting in the construction of numerous bikeways across the country.

European studies have shown significant decreases in accident rates on streets where bikeways have been physically separated from motor vehicles. American cities that have provided bikeway facilities have found that there are far more users than were initially expected.

There are three different classes of bikeways in common use. One type provides separate right-of-way for the exclusive use of bicycles; intersections with pedestrians and motor traffic are minimal. Another type restricts the rights-of-way exclusively for bicycles, but allows a greater number of crossovers for parking, driveways, etc. The last type consists of shared rights-of-way, with signs posted to indicate bike routes. The continuing awareness of the rights of cyclists is, indeed, good news.

National Safety Council's Rules Of The Road

A cyclist has the responsibility of ensuring his own safety, as well as the safety of others on the road. By adhering to the following rules, you will enjoy years of safe cycling.

1. Obey all applicable traffic regulations, signs, signals and markings.
2. Observe all local ordinances pertaining to bicycle operation.
3. Keep right, drive with traffic, not against it. Drive single file.
4. Watch out for drain grates, soft shoulders and other road surface hazards.
5. Watch out for car door opening, or for cars pulling into traffic.
6. Don't carry passengers or packages that interfere with your vision or control.
7. Never hitch a ride on a truck or other vehicle.
8. Be extremely careful at all intersections, particularly when making a left turn.
9. Use hand signals to indicate turning or stopping.
10. Protect yourself at night with the required reflectors and lights.
11. Drive a safe bike. Have it inspected to insure good mechanical condition.
12. Drive your bike defensively; watch out for the other guy.

One safety rule: Always ride single file!

Recommended Accessories

In general, the less one carries while bicycling, the better. However, there are times when setting out with nothing more than the machine underneath and the wind at your back simply isn't enough. Though accessories add weight to the total package and can slow you down or even throw you off balance (especially when carrying poorly designed or distributed items), sometimes the addition of a carrier or a bag, a horn or a water bottle can make cycling more enjoyable and convenient. It's often a matter of balancing weight against need.

Be Secure

The first accessory you'll need—whether you're an urban or rural cyclist—is some sort of security system.

You're paying good money for a bike. With thefts continuing to rise, it's only good sense that you protect your machine when you're away from it.

One important fact about a chain or cable: It's not going to deter the determined bike thief anymore than the spring lock on your front door will deter the professional burglar. It will serve to protect you from the casual thief and may discourage the pro from stealing your bike when the one that's parked next to it is easier picking.

If you're not convinced, consider this. There's a chain cutter on the market that will snip in a matter of seconds any chain or cable light enough to carry on a bike. It's not an inexpensive tool, so it's not likely that anyone but the professional bike thief will own one. Still, if you have a very expensive cycle that you prize

57

A cable and lock can be conveniently carried under the seat when not in use.

There are many different types of bag carriers available, including front and rear carriers.

highly, the best way to guard against its theft is not to leave it unguarded.

For those times when your bike must sit unwatched, buy a ⅜-inch plastic-coated cable (chains are heavier and costlier and offer no more protection). Use it with a hardened-shackle key lock. When not in use, this combo is light and compact enough to carry in a saddle bag or wrapped around the seat post.

Bells And Horns

If you do a lot of urban cycling—like on paths through city parks—you'll need a small bell or bulb horn to let pedestrians know you're coming. For street cycling, you'll want something that can be heard over the roar of an auto engine. That means a gas-powered horn (available at most cycle shops) with a volume loud enough to rival most car horns. Don't use this type of horn on a park lane or other thoroughfare where people are present, though, unless you enjoy startling and/or angering those pedestrians you're trying to avoid.

As an alternative to a signal system that requires removing at least one hand from the bars, consider a loud whistle on a chain. You can dangle it from your neck until you approach congested areas, at which time you can slip it between your lips and leave it there until the pathway clears. Also, on only mildly crowded pathways where you're cycling at a fairly slow pace, you might get by with words such as, "Bicycle on your right," or the like. But always assume the worst—that the pedestrian is likely to step right into your path. And

remember pedestrians have the right-of-way.

Bags And Carriers

Nearly every bike, in our opinion, should include as an accessory at least a rear, spring-type carrier. It bolts onto the seat and the rear axle to provide a sturdy rack for carting small objects conveniently. (Note: these carriers are not designed to support persons, and children especially should be heartily discouraged from riding "double" on any bike built for one.)

For serious touring, bolt-on bag holders are a good idea. If you carry a great amount of gear, there's little chance the bags can interfere with wheels or pedals. Although waterproof nylon bags with aluminum interior frames are by far the lightest add-ons for your bike, many tourers prefer the more durable, longer lasting waterproofed canvas construction. Again, it's a trade-off between weight and individual needs.

Although backpacks aren't generally recommended for cyclists, more and more people—especially students who find the convenience of carrying their packs with them throughout the day—are turning to them. If a backpack is necessary, choose a model that is designed to hang as low as possible on your back for best weight distribution. Also, skiers' belt packs are nice for cycling, although they don't carry as much as backpacks do. By all means, stay clear of hikers' frame packs, which cause a lot of wind resistance, reduce the cyclist's flexibility, and tend to be top-heavy. And never exceed 25 pounds of backpack weight; after that, steering and crosswind problems become serious.

If you plan to do any riding at night, a light is a necessary addition to your bicycle.

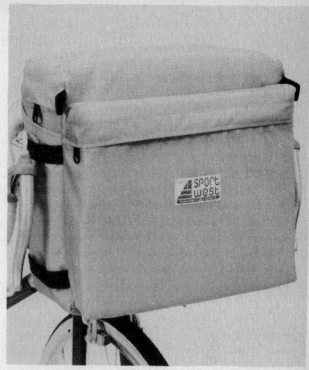

Even larger touring bags won't interfere with wheels and pedals if properly attached.

Lights

If you do any dim-light bicycling (including riding during dark storms), you should have a light on your bike. Its function isn't to enable you to see, but to be seen.

Generator-driven lights work only when the bike is moving. But then they don't use batteries, so they can't go "dead." On the other hand, about the most easily visible type of light is the battery-operated flashlight-type that straps to arm or leg. Not only does it throw a beam of light out, but it also jiggles and gyrates as your arm or leg moves up and down, providing excellent visibility to oncoming and up-coming cars. The model with dual bulbs is best.

Mirrors

The best type of mirror is the one that attaches to glasses or cap brim. Learn, as motorcyclists do, to look quickly over your shoulder in the direction you're turning and don't rely solely on any mirror.

Distance Meters

Odometers, or cyclometers, are useful and fun for keeping track of distance on short exercise runs or on long tours. They're easily installed and can be extremely accurate.

Pumps

This is a useless piece of equipment—until you have a

flat. Then, it suddenly becomes worth its weight in gold. Frame-mounted pumps are fine for touring (but be certain the pump connector and the valve of your tires are compatible). But you should also own a sturdy, foot-weighted model for use at home.

Water Bottles

Racers use lightweight plastic half-liter bottles—either one or two—to replenish the water they lose through perspiration. Tourists, too, find them useful when bicycling where no taverns, stores, or fountains are known to exist. But be forewarned: almost anything drunk from a plastic bottle tastes like plastic. If you have an alternative, use it.

Tool And Repair Kit

Either buy a specially made bike repair kit or make one up yourself. Include the finest quality tools you can afford. And include, too, a tube or tire patch kit as appropriate. A can of pressurized lubricant can be a welcome addition while on tour.

Helmets

For anyone who bicycles among auto traffic—whether heavy or light—this is an absolute must. The cyclist who fails to wear a helmet may not increase his chances of involvement in an auto-bike collision, but he'll likely increase his chances of not getting up and walking away.

The Bicycle Reviews

MULTI-SPEED DERAILLEUR BICYCLES

Schwinn World Sport 10-Speed

If you're looking for the fun and thrills of true lightweight cycling but also want an economical buy, this model should appeal to you. It's designed by Schwinn and built in Japan to the American manufacturer's specifications. That, in part, accounts for its lower than expected price. The frame is a rugged Schwinn-approved brazed and lugged construction of 18 gauge carbon steel (thus making it slightly heavier than some of Schwinn's more expensive X-tra Lite bicycle models). It features steel, drop-style handlebars and a black quilted racing-type saddle with a lightweight plastic base. The derailleurs are respectable—Maeda Sun Tour Honor (rear) and Maeda Sun Tour Spirit (front). The front hub is a Sunshine large-flange alloy; the rear, a Sunshine small-flange alloy. Shifters are Sun Tour handlebar stem mounted types, and brakes are aluminum alloy center-pull with extension levers (unspecified make). The rims are 27 × 1¼-inch tubular steel on which are mounted high-pressure gumwall tires of the same size. The crankset is the Silstar cotterless type with alloy crank arms and steel chainwheels. The frame sizes range from 19-inch (ladies') and 21-inch (men's) to 25-inch, and the weight of the bicycle is a medium-heavy 33 pounds with kickstand.
Approximate Retail Price: $156.95
Low Price: Not Available

Schwinn Continental

This is the top-of-the-line in Schwinn's 27-inch wheel, standard lightweight model line. It's a slightly heavier but smoother-riding bicycle favored by many tourists. Its frame is electro-forged, diamond-style of 16 gauge 1010 carbon steel with built-in kickstand housing and welded-on cable lugs. The handlebar is the SR Randonneur alloy

Schwinn's World Sport

drop style, and the saddle is a Schwinn-approved comfort-form racing style with vinyl cover over a specially molded pad. The derailleur is Schwinn-approved GT-510 with jam-free backpedal cage (rear) and Schwinn-approved GT-290 with special jam-free chain cage (front). Shifters are Schwinn-built Twin Stik fork, stem-mounted alloy type. The crankset is forged steel diamond style, heat treated crank and Schwinn patented 39 and 52-tooth chainwheels. Hubs are Schwinn-approved large-flange alloy with quick-release front. Tires are Schwinn High-Pressure Sports Touring gumwall, 27 × 1¼-inch, mounted on tubular steel chrome-plated rims of the same size. Brakes are Schwinn-approved alloy center-pull. Frame sizes range from 20 to 24 inches, and weight with kickstand is 36 pounds.

Approximate Retail Price: $201.95
Low Price: Not Available

Schwinn Deluxe Varsity 10-Speed

This model 10-speed, with slightly more weight than the Continental and at a slightly lower cost, is extremely popular for its easy shifting system. The frame is identically constructed to the Continental—electro-forged 16-gauge 1010 carbon steel with built-in kickstand housing and welded-on cable lugs. The handlebar is a Schwinn steel chrome plated, drop style, and the saddle is a Schwinn-approved comfort-form racing style with spring suspension and vinyl cover over specially molded pad—an unusual and unusually comfortable racing-style saddle. The derailleur is a Schwinn-approved Positron II (rear) and Schwinn-approved GT-290 (front). This model is equipped with the new Shimano FF system front freewheel and Positron II stem-mounted shifting lever which shifts into each gear speed with a positive click—both easy and convenient. The crankset is a Schwinn forged steel one-piece crank with 39 to 52-tooth chainwheels. Hubs are large-flange alloy (front) and small-flange alloy (rear);

Schwinn's Continental

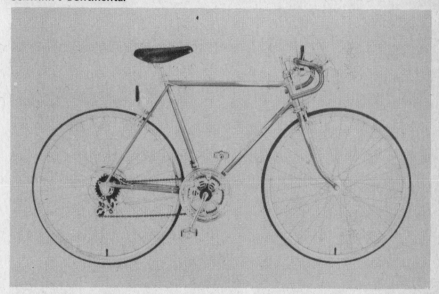

Schwinn's Deluxe Varsity

while brakes are Schwinn-approved alloy side-pull type with extension levers. Tires are Schwinn Breeze Sports Touring 27 × 1¼-inch gumwall mounted on tubular steel chrome-plated rims. The frame sizes range from 17 to 24 inches, and the weight with kickstand is 37 pounds.

Approximate Retail Price: $191.95
Low Price: Not Available

Schwinn Varsity Sport 10-Speed

Billed as America's best-selling full-size bicycle, the Varsity Sport is notable for its smooth and easy riding quality and rugged dependabil-

ity under a wide range of riding conditions. It features an electro-forged 16-gauge 1010 carbon steel frame with built-in kickstand housing and welded-on cable lugs. The handlebar is a Schwinn steel chrome-plated, drop-style model, and the saddle is a Schwinn-approved comfort-form racing style with vinyl cover over a special molded pad. Derailleur is the Schwinn-approved GT-510 (rear) and the Schwinn-approved GT-290 (front), and shifting levers are Schwinn Twin-Stik, fork stem mounted, alloy. The crankset is a Schwinn forged steel diamond-style heat-treated crank with 39 to

Schwinn's Varsity Sport

Schwinn's Suburban Tourist

outer chainguards. The freewheel is the Schwinn-approved FF system with 14-17-20-24-28-teeth cogs (10-speed only), and 14-17-21-26-32-teeth cogs (5-speed only). The hubs are Schwinn-approved small-flange alloy, front and rear. The brakes are Schwinn-approved alloy, side-pull style. The tires are Schwinn puff gumwall, 27 × 1¼-inches, mounted on Schwinn tubular steel 27 × 1¼-inch rims. Frame sizes range from 17-inch to 24-inch on both the 5- and 10-speed models. The weight is 39 pounds with the kickstand.
Approximate Retail Price: $192.95
Low Price: Not Available

Schwinn Le Tour 10-Speed

One of the finest mass-produced bicycles in its price range, this model has many quality features usually associated with more expensive bicycles. The frame is Schwinn's X-tra Lite fully brazed and lugged 18-gauge 1020 carbon steel. The handlebars are SR alloy, Randonneur drop-style. The saddle is an Avocet Touring II with leather-finish vinyl top and lightweight plastic base. The front derailleur is the GT 295 with two-piece chain cage for jam-free, positive shifting; the rear derailleur is the Shimano 400 Series. Shifting levers are Schwinn Twin Stik, stem mounted. The crankset is a durable Sugino Super Maxi alloy cotterless chainwheel with guard and chrome-molybdenum steel spindle. Brakes are forged alloy, center-pull style. Hubs are Maillard large-flange alloy with quick-release front for easy-off operation. The tires are Schwinn's high-pressure Sports Touring gumwall, 27 × 1¼-inch, mounted on UKAI narrow-section 27 × 1¼-inch rims, the weakest link in an otherwise impressive machine. The frame sizes range from 21 to 24 inches, and the weight is 30 pounds. A very respectable bicycle and a Consumer Guide® best buy for the money.
Approximate Retail Price: $221.95
Low Price: Not Available

52-tooth chainwheels. Hubs are Schwinn-approved large-flange alloy (front) and small-flange alloy (rear). The brakes are Schwinn-approved alloy side-pull types with extension levers. Tires are Schwinn Puff gumwall 27 × 1¼ inches mounted on tubular steel chrome-plated rims. Frame sizes range from 17 to 26 inches. Weight is a heavy 38 pounds.
Approximate Retail Price: $181.95
Low Price: Not Available

Schwinn Suburban Tourist 10-Speed and 5-Speed

Here's a basic short-distance bicycle built with conventional upright handlebars, yet it features low rolling resistance tires on a full adult-size 27-inch wheel. The frame is Schwinn electro-forged of 16-gauge 1010 carbon steel with built-in kickstand housing and welded-on cable lugs. The handlebar is a Schwinn chrome-plated steel upright tourist style with Schwinn patented cushion grips. The saddle is a Schwinn-approved mattress style with spring cushioning—this, combined with the touring bars, can prove uncomfortable over long rides. The derailleur is the Positron II positive-indexing (rear) and Schwinn-approved GT-290 (front) on the 10-speed model. Shifters are the exclusive Shimano Positron II fork stem mounted. The crankset is a Schwinn-approved forged steel one-piece crank with FF front freewheeling single plateau, 46-tooth chainwheel with inner and

Schwinn Super Le Tour 12-Speed **Best Buy**

Take the Le Tour and upgrade it with self-centering rear derailleur with six-cog cassette freewheel, downtube shifters, and several additional high-quality features, and you end up with a positive best buy in a lightweight touring bicycle. The frame is Schwinn's X-tra Lite torch-brazed, fully lugged 18-gauge 1020 carbon steel. Handlebars are SR alloy, Randonneur drop style. The saddle is Avocet Condor contour with leather finish vinyl top and lightweight plastic base (we recommend replacing the saddle with a leather model for added comfort on long-distance tours). The front and rear derailleurs are Shimano Altus LT Deluxe, and shifters work smoothly against the derailleurs: they're Shimano Altus LT Deluxe alloy downtube style. The crankset is a Sugino Super Maxi alloy cotterless chainwheel with chrome-molybdenum steel spindle. The brakes are the very positive Weinmann 605 Deluxe alloy side-pull, another step above the Le Tour. Hubs are Shimano's alloy small-flange free with quick-release (rear) and Schwinn-approved alloy small-flange with quick-release and wheel retention (front). Rims are impressive: Weinmann A-125 light alloy 27 × 1¼-inch on which are mounted Schwinn Super Record gumwall high-pressure 27 × 1¼-inch tires. Frame sizes range from 21 to 25 inches, and the weight is 28 pounds. Though some long-distance tourers find this weight too heavy for their liking, the quality components and on-road handling make this an impressive machine for the money—and a Consumer Guide® best buy.

Approximate Retail Price: $291.95
Low Price: Not Available

Schwinn Traveler 10-Speed **Best Buy**

This very popular, attractively priced, medium-weight touring bicycle is a good bet for people on a budget intent upon discovering the

Schwinn's Le Tour

Schwinn's Traveler

joys and health of touring. The frame is a fully lugged and brazed, 18-gauge 1020 carbon steel type; there's a steel Randonneur drop-style handlebar. The saddle is an Ariake black vinyl top with lightweight nylon base. Hubs are Shimano semi-large flange (front) and small-flange steel (rear). Front and rear derailleurs are the positive Shimano 400. Shift lever is the Shimano handlebar stem-mount type. Crankset consists of a Silstar 3-piece cotterless with alloy crank arms, chrome-molybdenum spindle, and chainguard. Brakes are Schwinn-approved center-pull type made of alloy. Tires are Schwinn Puff gumwall, 27 × 1¼-

inches, mounted on Araya steel rims of the same size—a definite drawback over alloy rims, adding weight where it's needed least. The frame sizes range from 19 to 25 inches. The weight is 32 pounds, too heavy for serious long-distance touring, but suitable for shorter trips. For the money, the Traveler 10-Speed is a Consumer Guide® best buy.

Approximate Retail Price: $181.95
Low Price: Not Available

Schwinn Deluxe Cruiser 5-Speed **Best Buy**

Schwinn has updated the old balloon-tire bike that has been so

Schwinn's Deluxe Cruiser

Motobecane's Mirage

popular for heavy-duty, multi-terrain cycling, with a 5-speed derailleur and hand brakes. The frame is Schwinn's electro-forged cantilever (which translates into *heavy*). The Deluxe Cruiser 5 features a Maillard internal expander rear hub, a chrome-plated steel front hub, a heavy-duty saddle, and heavy-duty, .105 spokes. The crank, too, is built to last, of heat-treated forged steel. Tubular steel rims, available in either 24- or 26-inch sizes, on which are mounted 2.125-inch tractor tires translates into a soft, comfortable ride. A wide-base upright handlebar and chrome fenders make this a smart-looking, extremely durable machine, the type that earned Schwinn the nickname, "The Cadillac of Bicycles." It should last forever. The approximate weight is 45 pounds. This bicycle is also available as a one-speed, coaster-brake model called the Cruiser. The extremely durable construction and

thoughtful design combine with low cost to make this bike a Consumer Guide® best buy.
Approximate Retail Price: $198.95
Low Price: Not Available

Motobecane Mirage 10-Speed

This bicycle is a dependable touring machine that's popular for short tours, with students, and for general purpose commuting. It's a medium-priced touring machine made in France with sturdy yet lightweight frame and quality components. The frame is a fully lugged and brazed 2040 high-resiliency steel tubing type, with brazed-on cable guides. The handlebar is a Motobecane randonneur drop-style. The saddle is a well-padded Touring "Record E." Hubs are Shimano 400 with quick-release front, and Shimano 800 with Allen nuts rear. Derailleurs are Huret Club-Driver. Shift levers are stem-mounted rachet type. Brakes are Weinmann 501 with

Yoshigi safety levers. The crankset is a Selecta T 39 to 52 double chainwheel with built-in chain-guard. The tires are Motobecane-Hutchinson high-pressure gumwall mounted on chrome-plated Rigida 27 × 1¼-inch rims. The pedals are the popular and durable Lyotard 136R, chrome-plated with safety reflectors. Frame sizes range from 19½ to 25 inches. The weight is 28 pounds.
Approximate Retail Price: $245.00
Low Price: $220.00

Motobecane Grand Sprint 10-Speed

Designed to appeal to the junior or beginning racer, this model is the most affordable training bicycle in Motobecane's lineup. It offers a wider gear ratio and responsive handling. It's a sleek, well-designed and attractive sport cycle that even the serious tourer will appreciate. It features a fully

Motobecane's Grand Sprint

Motobecane's Nomade

lugged and brazed Huret 888 frame with Motobecane "racing bend" (drop-bar style) handlebars. The saddle is a training padded type. The derailleurs are Shimano Altus LT, both front and rear. Shift levers are of the downtube variety. The crankset consists of SI 50LA EL, 40 to 52 double chainwheel; the chain is a Uniglide. Hubs are Shimano 800 with Allen nuts, both front and rear. Brakes are the excellent Weinmann 501 side-pull type with quick release and drilled alloy levers. The tires are the impressively lightweight, tight-gripping Pirelli 27 × 1-inch VL78 high-pressure, offering extremely low rolling resistance and excellent gripping. The pedals are Union "631 RU" racing type, alloy, with toe clips and reflectors. The frame sizes range from 19½ to 25 inches, and the weight is 26 pounds. The impressive credentials of this bicycle for the beginning-to-serious racer, as well as the long-distance tourer, marks it as a Consumer Guide® best buy.

Approximate Retail Price: $285.00
Low Price: $245.00

Motobecane Nomade 10-Speed

This is a bicycle with a fully lugged, 2040 high-resiliency tube frame featuring brazed-on cable guides and racing rear tips. The handlebars are Motobecane randonneur drop-style with cotton tape and plugs, and the saddle is a touring "Record E," padded. The derailleur is the Huret Club II (front) and the Huret Driver (rear) with stem

shifters. The rear cluster is either Maillard or Maeda 5-speed, 14 to 28, black. The crankset is the SR "SI 5 SDZ" 40 to 52 double chainwheel with CG III alloy chainguard. Hubs are Normandy alloy (front) and Atom alloy (rear). Brakes are Motobecane center-pull with safety levers, considerably less impressive than the Weinmann and Campagnolo models on other Motobecane bicycles. Tires are Motobecane-Hutchinson high-pressure gumwall with Schrader valve mounted on 27 × 1¼-inch Rigida chrome-plated rims. Pedals are Union chrome-plated with safety reflectors. Frame sizes range from 19½ to 25 inches, and weight is 28½ pounds.

Approximate Retail Price: $179.00
Low Price: $161.00

Motobecane Nomade Sprint 12-Speed

For a few dollars more than the Nomade, the Nomade Sprint offers quite a bit more quality in component parts. It's an excellent bicycle for the young cyclist who appreciates the advantages of a lightweight machine. The frame is a fully lugged 2040 high-resiliency tube with brazed-on cable guides and racing rear tips. The handlebars are Motobecane randonneur-type (drop-style) with cotton tape. Saddle is the touring "Record E," padded. The derailleurs are Shimano Altus ST/RS front and rear, a step up from the Nomade. Shifters are stem type. The

crankset consists of Shimano's 400 "Selecta B," 30 to 52 double chainwheels and alloy chain guard. The chain is either Sedis or Izumi, black. Hubs both front and rear are Shimano 400 low-flange, and brakes are Weinmann 730 side-pull type with alloy safety levers, another step up over the Nomade. Tires on the Sprint are 27 × 1¼-inch Motobecane high-pressure gumwall with Schrader valve mounted on Rigida chrome-plated rims of the same size. The frame sizes range from 19½ to 25 inches, and the weight is 27½ pounds—slightly lighter than the Nomade.

Approximate Retail Price: $199.00
Low Price: $179.00

Motobecane Grand Touring 10-Speed

This lightweight and attractive touring cycle is very popular because of many quality features, like a lightweight frame with heat-treated tubes that eliminate incipient fatigue cracking under stress; longer oval chain-stays which lengthen the bicycle for accessory rear fenders; and top quality brakes and derailleurs. The frame of this touring cycle is of double butted Vitus 172 with brazed-on cable guides. The handlebar is the Motobecane randonneur drop-style alloy with "M" engraving, soft sleeves with lever hoods. Saddle is the Italia "Anatomic" leather-like top. The derailleurs are Sun Tour SL (front) and Sun Tour V-GT Luxe (rear) with downtube ratchet shifters. The

Motobecane's Nomade Sprint

Motobecane's Grand Touring

Motobecane's Grand Record

Motobecane's Team Champion

19½ to 25 inches, and weight is a light 25½ pounds.
Approximate Retail Price: $294.00
Low Price: $265.00

Motobecane Grand Record 12-Speed

This lightweight cycle is excellent for both touring and racing, especially for the young competitive racer. It's equipped with many full-out racing components and is an extremely handsome machine. It features a frame of double-butted Vitus 172 tubing with brazed-on cable guides, racing rear stays, and Huret tips with adjusters. The handlebar is the Belleri alloy Competition with soft sleeves, and the saddle is the San Marco Competition model with skin leather top. Also impressive are the lightweight Shimano 600 EX (both front and rear) derailleurs with downtube shifters. The rear cluster is the Shimano 600 EX 6-speed; and the crankset boasts Shimano's 600 EX 40 to 52 chainwheels. The chain is the Uniglide in attactive gold finish. Hubs are Shimano 600 EX low-flange with quick release, both front and rear. The brakes are Shimano 600 X side-pull models with quick release and drilled alloy levers with hoods. The tires are low-rolling-resistance 700 C Clement "Gentleman," high-pressure with Presta valve mounted on 700 C Rigida 13/20 alloy rims with spoke protectors. Frame sizes range from 21 to 25 inches, and the weight is a light, responsive 22½ pounds.
Approximate Retail Price: $419.00
Low Price: $380.00

Motobecane Team Champion 12-Speed

Motobecane's finest racing machine, this model is one you'll not have to drill-out to bear-off unnecessary weight, as on some manufacturers' models. It's a racing machine designed to be the lightest, most agile piece of equipment you can buy—an impressive combination of frame construction and components. The frame of the Team Champion is

crankset is the SR "SI 5 DRG AH," 40 to 52 double chainwheels with alloy chain guard. The chain is either Sedis or Izumi in a rich-looking black finish. Pedals are Atom 440 alloy barrel with safety reflectors. Hubs featured are the Normandy alloy large-flange, quick release, both front and rear. Brakes are the impressive Weinmann Vainqueur 999 center-pull with safety levers and quick release. The tires Motobecane chose for this touring cycle are the very impressive 27 × 1-inch Pirelli VL78 high-pressure gumwalls mounted on 27 × 1¼-inch Pellet Super Champion competition alloy lightweight rims—a superb combination offering durability and lightness, something to be appreciated on a long tour. Frame sizes range from

double-butted Columbus (8 tubes) with double-tapered seat stays. It features brazed-on cable guides and derailleur cable tunnels with forged Campagnolo tips and adjusters. The handlebar is the light, durable Cinelli 66 with cotton tape and plugs, while the saddle is the impressive Italia "Super Leggera" suede top. The derailleur is the Campagnolo Record with downtube shifters; the rear cluster is the Cyclo Pan 6-speed in black, and the crankset consists of the Campy 4030 Super Record 42 to 53 double chainwheels. The chain is the gold Sedis Sedicolor. Pedals, too, are impressive: the Campagnolo 1037 A Record with alloy barrel and black cage and Christophe Z toe clips and straps. The hubs are Campagnolo 1034 Record, low-flange, both front and rear. Tires are the 700 C Clement Paris-Ronbaix tubular, puncture-free, mounted on 700 C Pellet Arc En Ciel alloy rims with chrome-plated spoke and spoke protectors. Frame sizes range from 21 to 25 inches, and the weight is a super responsive, light 20½ pounds.
Approximate Retail Price: $959.00
Low Price: Not Available

*Univega Sportour 12-Speed

This is a quick, sporty, and elegant 12-speed machine of Italian design, built with chrome-molybdenum main tubing and fitted with highly selected alloy components like a cotterless crankset with interchangeable chainrings and quick-release hubs with cassette clusters for the finest response with durable performance. It has a fully lugged, chrome-molybdenum 4140 lightweight frame and Sakae alloy racing-bend handlebars. The saddle is the Univega Touring Padded with Sakae CT-P6 milled alloy, black-anodized seatpost. The hubs are Shimano alloy, small-flange with quick release, both front and rear. Derailleurs are the popular Shimano Altus LT (front) with downtube shifters and the Shimano HF 400 Uniglide (rear) for fast, sure shifting of gears. Brakes are the Dia-Compe 500G side-pull model. Araya light-weight anodized alloy

rims measure 27 × 1¼ inches. The tires are the Univega Gran Sport high-pressure, also 27 × 1¼ inches. The crankset features Sakae cotterless alloy with removable chainring. Pedals are the Sakae SP-400 alloy body with rattrap. Frame sizes range from 19½ to 25 inches, and the weight is a medium light 26 pounds.
Approximate Retail Price: $239.95
Low Price: Not Available

* The Italian-manufactured Univega bicycles are currently available only on the West Coast and in Massachusetts, but should be available nationwide within a year or two.

Univega Gran Turismo 15-Speed   **Best Buy**

This bicycle is a good example of what a lightweight Grand Touring machine should be. It has 15 speeds for negotiating any terrain, a wide gearing ratio with a beautifully designed lightweight frame and fork, fitted with impressive components. It's one of the most attractive bicycles around, with its distinctive gold chain and professional-looking Classic Gold frame. It features a fully lugged, chrome-molybdenum 4140 lightweight steel frame and handlebar of the Sakae, randonneur-type drop style. The saddle is the comfortable and long-wearing Univega 77C-DX Touring model. Hubs are Sunshine MS-80 large-flange, of the quick-release design. Derailleurs are Sun Tour VX and Sun Tour Pro-Compe. Shift levers are of the downtube variety. Brakes are Dia-Compe 610 centerpull, which grip positively the Araya light alloy, anodized 27 × 1¼-inch rims. Tires are Univega Gran Sport 27 × 1⅛-inch high-pressure. The crankset consists of a Sakae cotterless forged alloy, 5-pin Spider and removable, three-alloy chainring. Pedals are the Sakae SP-300 with alloy body. The chain is the Shimano 600 Uniglide with gold-and-black finish. The frame sizes range from 19½-25 inches, and the weight is 26½ pounds. This machine proves that a bicycle can feature thoughtful engineering and quality component parts—and still be attractive. At its surprisingly low

retail price, Consumer Guide® rates it a best buy.
Approximate Retail Price: $265.00
Low Price: Not Available

Univega Nuovo Sport 10-Speed

This model is a beautifully detailed, well constructed bicycle that is slightly heavy for long touring, yet a good buy in multi-speed machines. It features a high-tension, fully lugged 1024 steel tubing frame and a handlebar of heavy steel, racing bend type. The saddle is the Univega Touring, padded. The derailleurs are the Sun Tour VGT Luxe both front and rear, and shifters are the UB 10 stem-type. The crankset is SR Silstar cotterless, alloy crank, 40 to 52 alloy chainwheels with guard. Hubs are Sunshine's alloy, large-flange with quick release both front and rear. Brakes are the Dia-Compe, center-pull style with extension levers. Tires are Univega's Sport, 27 × 1¼ inches, mounted on Araya narrow steel H. P. of the same size. Alloy rims would make the bicycle somewhat lighter and should be considered as an alternate. Frame sizes range from 19½ to 25 inches. Also available in 19-inch size with 26 × 1¼-inch wheels. Weight is a somewhat hefty 29½ pounds.
Approximate Retail Price: $179.95
Low Price: Not Available

Univega Viva Sport 10-Speed

This attractive machine is an excellent touring bike. The frame is of high-tension 1024 butted steel tubing, fully lugged with spoon-type stay ends. The handlebar is a steel racing-bend type, and the saddle is the Univega Touring, padded. Derailleurs are the Sun Tour VGT Luxe with downtube shifter. The crankset is the SR Silstar alloy cotterless crank, 40 to 52 chainwheels with guard. Hubs are Sunshine's alloy, small-flange with quick-release front. Brakes are Dia-Compe, side-pull type with extension levers. Tires on this model are the Univega Gran Sport, 27 × 1⅛-inch high-pressure for low rolling resistance mounted on Araya light alloy, anodized 27 × 1¼-inch rims.

The frame sizes range from 19½ to 25 inches, and the weight—due greatly to the alloy rims, is a respectable 27½ pounds, a full two pounds lighter than the steel-rimmed Nuovo Sport.
Approximate Retail Price: $205.00
Low Price: Not Available

Univega Super Ten 10-Speed

This is a very good buy in a heavy "lightweight," yet durable, 10-speed cycle. It features a frame made of light steel tubing, fully lugged, and a Univega Tubular fork with chrome-plated tips. The handlebar is steel of the racing bend style (substituting an alloy bar may lighten the bicycle by more than a pound). The saddle is a padded racing type. Derailleurs are the Sun Tour-Seven with stem shifters, adequate for a bicycle in this price class, with stem-mounted shifters. The crankset is SR Silstar alloy with cotterless crank and alloy disc guard. The hubs are Shimano alloy, large-flange, both front and rear. Brakes are Dia-Compe, center-pull style, with extension levers; alloy-constructed. Tires are 27 × 1¼-inch high-pressure gumwall mounted on chrome-plated steel rims (again, consider replacing with alloy rims for lighter rolling weight) measuring 27 × 1¼

inches. Frame sizes range from 19½ to 25 inches. Weight is a heavy 32 pounds.
Approximate Retail Price: $154.95
Low Price: Not Available

Univega Custom Ten 10-Speed

This is a rugged 10-speed machine for the young cyclist on a low budget. It features a light steel tubing frame, fully lugged, with handlebar of steel, racing-bend style. The fork is Univega's tubular with chrome-plated tips, and the saddle is a padded racing type. Derailleurs are Sun Tour or Shimano RS with stem shifters. The crankset is forged steel, cottered with C.P. disc guard—expected in a bicycle in this price class. However, the cycle can be ordered with Shimano's FF alloy system, which is recommended. Pedals are steel racing type with safety reflectors. Hubs are large-flange steel, which add to the overall weight of the machine. Brakes are Dia-Compe, side-pull type, of alloy and with extension levers. The tires are standard 27 × 1¼-inch high-pressure gumwall mounted on chrome-plated steel rims of the same size. Frame sizes range from 19½ to 25 inches, and the weight is a rather formidable 33 pounds—but substituting alloy

components for steel wherever possible will add a little to the price while adding a lot of overall performance by reducing rolling weight.
Approximate Retail Price: $134.95
Low Price: Not Available

Univega Super Star 10-Speed

This mini-version of an adult 10-speed cycle is predictably heavy, with very little alloy and a great deal of steel comprising its components. The frame is light steel tubing, fully lugged, with a Univega tubular fork with chrome plated tips. The handlebar is steel, racing-bend style, and the saddle is a padded racing type. Derailleurs are Sun Tour or Shimano RS with stem shifters. The crankset is forged steel, cottered, with C.P. disc guard. Pedals are steel of the racing type with safety reflectors. Hubs are large-flange steel. Brakes are Dia-Compe, side-pull alloy, with extension levers—one of the few component parts not adding excessive weight to the cycle. The tires are a child's-size 24 × 1⅜ inches, gumwall, mounted on chrome-plated steel rims measuring 24 × 1⅜ inches. Frame sizes are 18½ inches in boys' style, and 16½ inches in girls' "mixte" (semi-dropped tube) style. Weight is 32 pounds.
Approximate Retail Price: $134.95
Low Price: Not Available

Univega Gran Premio 12-Speed

This model has a classic touring look that's sure to appeal to most every cyclist who's ever pedaled along the roadway. It's specially designed and hand built to be a machine *par excellence* in its class. And its light weight makes it an excellent bicycle for racing. It features a hand-built frame with double-butted chrome molybdenum 4140 tubing, tapered rear stays, brazed-on cable guide, and other accessories. The fork is high-tension 1024 tubular, chrome-plated Italian Racing Style Crown Mod C5. The handlebar is the Nitto Universal with racing bend. The saddle is the Univega top-quality suede Racing with Sakae CT-P5B

Raleigh's Professional MKV

milled alloy, black-anodized seatpost. Derailleurs are Sun Tour Cyclone with Superb downtube controls. The crankset features Sakae SAX-5LAEL, cotterless forged alloy chainwheels; chain is Sun Tour's Ultra 6 with black-and-silver finish. Pedals are the popular Sakae SP-100AL light alloy with alloy toe clips and leather straps. Hubs are Sunshine Gyro-Master forged alloy, small-flange with quick-release. Brakes are the impressive and sure-gripping New Gran-Compe GC-500 side-pull with allen type center bolt. Tires are Univega Superlight 700C × 25C high-pressure (100 pounds) with French valve tubes mounted on Araya 20 A 700C polished light alloy tubular Hallow Pattern rims, both lightweight and durable. Frame sizes range from 21 to 25 inches in classic gold finish. The weight is 23 pounds.

Approximate Retail Price: $420.00
Low Price: Not Available

Raleigh Professional MKV 12-Speed

For the serious tourer who expects to pay for the best, the Raleigh Professional MKV offers high-quality components and refined engineering in a smart-looking package. The frame is fully lugged and double-butted, made of durable, light-weight Reynolds 531 tubular alloy, and the fork is Reynolds 531 taper-gauge with Vagner crown and Campagnolo fork ends for excellent response and liveliness. The handlebar is Raleigh's Engraved light alloy, and the saddle is the highly regarded Brooks Professional Team Special. Hubs are Campagnolo Nuovo Record, small-flange with quick-release both front and rear. Derailleurs include the famed Campagnolo Record (front) with downtube shifters and Campagnolo Nuovo Record (rear). The crankset is Campagnolo Nuovo record cotterless alloy, 42 to 51-tooth chainwheels. The chain is the Sedis Sedicolor. Pedals are Campagnolo's Super Leggera Strada. Brakes are the very responsive Campy Record Short-Reach, cen-

ter-pull variety, which grip quickly, quietly, and surely. Tires are Raleigh Imperforable Seta mounted on Mavic Sprint rims with reinforcing ferrules. Extras include Silca Impero air pump, Christophe toe clips and Brooks toe straps, brazed-on downtube tunnel clip, stops and bottle cage bosses, and chrome-plated fork tips both front and rear. Frame sizes range from 20½ to 25½ inches, and weight is a light, responsive 23 pounds. Obviously not a bicycle for everyone, this machine features only the highest quality components assembled with care. The serious cyclist should find years of reliable cycling. It's a Consumer Guide® best buy.

Approximate Retail Price: $925.00
Low Price: Not Available

Rampar Superbe 12-Speed

This beautiful and responsive touring machine has an attractive gold finish frame of Tange chrome-molybdenum, double-butted and fully lugged, for durability and lightness. The fork is the Tange Taper-Gauge with sloping crown and Sun Tour Superbe fork ends. Handlebar is engraved light alloy. The saddle is the comfortable Rampar padded suede on a light-

weight nylon base. Hubs are Sun Tour Superbe, small-flange, with quick-release. Front and rear derailleurs are Sun Tour Superbe with downtube shifters. Brakes are Sun Tour Superbe side-pull variety, which grip the Araya alloy rims with reinforcing ferrules cleanly and firmly. The crankset is the Sun Tour Superbe cotterless alloy, 42 to 52-tooth chainwheels. Chain is Sun Tour's Ultra 6. Tires are Raleigh's Nylon Extra lightweight. Extras include toe clips and straps, brazed-on cable guides, downtube tunnel clip, shift lever bosses, bottle bosses, and bottle cage. Frame sizes range from 21½ to 25½ inches, and the weight is a light 23 pounds. For its light weight and quality construction, Consumer Guide® rates this a best buy.

Approximate Retail Price: $619.00
Low Price: Not Available

Raleigh Competition G.S. 10-Speed

Another impressive model from the Raleigh lineup of lightweight cycles, this features a frame of Reynolds 531 doubled-butted tubing and stays with Campagnolo fork ends. The fork is a Reynolds 531 Taper-Gauge with Vagner-crown and Campagnolo G.S. fork ends. The handlebar is the Raleigh

Rampar's Superbe

Italienne alloy, randonneur drop style. The saddle is the Brooks Professional, both comfortable and efficient, of fine-grade leather. The derailleurs are Campagnolo Gran sport (rear) and Campagnolo Gran Sport (front) with downtube shifter controls. The crankset is the Campy Gran Sport cotterless alloy, 42 to 52-tooth chainwheels, with a freewheel of 13 to 24 teeth by Maillard. The chain is unspecified. Pedals are Campagnolo Gran Sport. Hubs are Campagnolo Gran Sport, small-flange with quick-release both front and rear. Brakes are the impressive Weinmann 605 alloy side-pulls with wheel guides. Tires are Raleigh's 700c × 25c

Skinside mounted on Weinmann 700c alloy concave A124 Narrow Section rims. Extras include competition air pump, Brooks toe straps and Christophe toe clips, brazed-on rear gear stop, chrome-plated stays and fork blades. Frame sizes range from 21½ to 25½ inches, and weight is only 24 pounds.

Approximate Retail Price: $499.00
Low Price: Not Available

Rampar Touring 14 14-Speed

Best Buy

The unique 7-speed freewheel on this Sun Tour-equipped bicycle

makes it a true touring machine suitable for tackling nearly any terrain. The frame is of Tange high-tensile double-butted tubes and stays. The fork is Tange's Taper-Gauge with forged crown and Sun Tour G.S. ends. The handlebar is the light SR alloy, randonneur turn-down style, and the saddle is the Rampar Padded Suede on a light-weight nylon base. The derailleurs consist of Sun Tour's VX-GT (rear) and Sun Tour VX (front) with handlebar-end shifters. The crank-set is Sun Tour VX cotterless alloy, 39 to 52-tooth chainwheels. Chain is the Sun Tour Ultra 6. Hubs are Sun Tour Road VX, large-flange and quick-release both front and rear. Brakes are the Dia-Compe Cantilever with drilled levers and natural gum rubber hoods. Pedals are Sun Tour's Road VX light alloy. Tires are Raleigh's 700c × 25c Skinside mounted on Araya 700c alloy rims. Extras include rigid light alloy front and rear carriers, toe clips and straps, brazed-on cable guides and water bottle cage bosses. Frame sizes range from 21½ to 25½ inches. The weight is 28 pounds. An excellent bicycle for the serious tourer, this model comes with many standard features which other cycles lack—and at a competitive price—making it a Consumer Guide® best buy.

Approximate Retail Price: $399.00
Low Price: Not Available

Raleigh's Competition GS

Rampar's Touring 14

Raleigh Super Course 12-Speed

For the rider who wants good performance at a moderate price, this cycle features a short wheel base for quick response (and a somewhat rough ride—you can't have everything). It has a Reynolds 531 alloy frame construction with Raleigh 20 to 30 High Tensile Steel stays and Sun Tour G. S. fork ends. The handlebar is the Raleigh Italienne alloy, and the saddle is a suede top over a nylon base for comfort and long wear. The derailleurs are Sun Tour VX-GT (rear) and Sun Tour VX (front) with 12-speed handlebar end shifters. The crankset is the Raleigh/SR alloy 5-pin cotterless, 42 to 52-tooth chain-

wheels with Allen Key bolts; the freewheel is the Sun Tour Ultra 6, and the chain is Sun Tour Ultra 6. Hubs are Atom small-flange quick release. Pedals: SR Sp 100 AL alloy. Brakes are the very fine Weinmann 500 short reach side-pull model with quick release. Tires are Raleigh 700c gumwall high-pressure mounted on Weinmann 700c alloy concave A124 narrow section rims. Extras include Brooks toe straps and Christophe toe clips, brazed-on cable eyes, arch, guides, downtube stops, and chrome-plated fork tips. Frame sizes range from 21½ to 25½ inches. Weight is 26 pounds.
Approximate Retail Price: $339.00
Low Price: Not Available

Raleigh Super Grand Prix 10-Speed

Best Buy

This is a very good machine that is lightweight and boasts some fine component parts. It's a no-frills bicycle built for touring. It has a Raleigh 20 to 30 High Tensile Steel frame and a Raleigh 20 to 30 High Tensile Steel with Forged Vagner crown fork. The handlebar is the Raleigh Maes alloy, and the saddle is imitation suede top on a padded nylon base. The derailleur is the Raleigh/Sun Tour VGT (rear) and the Raleigh/Sun Tour Compe V (front) with handlebar-end shifters so gears can be changed without removing hands from the bar. The crankset is the Raleigh/SR alloy, 5-pin cotterless, 42 to 52-tooth chainwheels with slotted spider and Allen Key bolts. The freewheel is the Raleigh/Sun Tour Perfect, 14 to 34 teeth. Pedals are Atom's 440 alloy. Hubs are Normandy large-flange alloy with quick-release. Brakes are Raleigh/Weinmann short-reach alloy center-pull style with quick release and extension levers. The tires are Raleigh 700c gumwall high-pressure on Raleigh 700c alloy rims. Extras include Brooks toe straps and Christophe toe clips, brazed-on cable eyes, arch, guide, and downtube stops. The frame sizes range from 20½ to 25½ inches, and the weight is 26 pounds. For the serious tourer not looking to spend more money than

Raleigh's Super Course

Raleigh's Super Grand Prix

necessary, Consumer Guide® rates this bicycle a best buy.
Approximate Retail Price: $269.00
Low Price: Not Available

Raleigh Grand Prix

This Super Grand Prix look-alike is the twin of its namesake except for a few small details—and a lower price tag. The Grand Prix is heavier and somewhat slower rolling, which can be a disappointment on long tours. But it offers relatively high quality and dependable craftsman-ship at a reasonable price. This model features a Raleigh 20 to 30 High Tensile Steel frame and Raleigh 20 to 30 High Tensile Steel with forged Vagner crown fork. The handlebar is the Raleigh Maes alloy, and the saddle is a padded vinyl top on a lightweight nylon base. The derailleurs are Raleigh/Sun Tour VGT (rear) and Raleigh/Sun Tour Compe V (front) with handlebar-mounted stem power shifters. The crankset is the Raleigh/SR alloy, 5-pin cotterless, 42 to 52-tooth chainwheels. Freewheel is the Raleigh/Sun Tour

Peugeot's U09 Grand Sport

Perfect with 14 to 34 teeth. Pedals are Raleigh ball bearing with safety reflectors, a step down from the Atom 440 alloy pedals on the Super GP. Hubs are Normandy's large-flange alloy with quick release. Brakes are the Raleigh/Weinmann alloy center-pull with quick release and extension levers. Tires are the Raleigh 27 × 1¼-inch high-pressure gumwall mounted on 27 × 1¼-inch chrome-plated steel. This last feature adds approximately two pounds to the weight of this model over the Super Grand Prix. Extras include brazed-on cable eyes, arch, guides, and downtube stops, chrome-plated front fork blades. Frame sizes range from 19¾ to 25½ inches; weight is 29 pounds.
Approximate Retail Price: $239.00
Low Price: Not Available

Raleigh Record Ace 10-Speed

Here's a competitively priced model that's designed with Raleigh-branded component parts and built to be durable. It's the heaviest of the Raleigh models reviewed here, but still light enough for short touring and commuting and an excellent first multi-speed bike for a youngster. It has a frame of Raleigh 20 to 30 High Tensile

Steel and a fork of Raleigh 20 to 30 High Tensile Steel with a pressed box crown. The handlebar is a Raleigh Maes alloy, and the Saddle is a Brooks CR3. Derailleurs are Raleigh/Sun Tour VGT (rear) and Raleigh/Sun Tour Compe V (front) with handlebar-mounted stem power shifters. The crankset consists of the Raleigh/SR alloy, 5-pin cotterless 42 to 52-tooth chainwheels. Freewheel is the Raleigh/Sun Tour Perfect 14 to 34 teeth. Hubs are Normandy large-flange alloy, with a quick-release front. Pedals are Raleigh ball bearing with safety reflectors. The seat post is of chrome-plated steel, where other Raleigh models use alloy—a fact that adds an even pound to the Record Ace over the Grand Prix, its nearest competitor feature-for-feature. Brakes are Raleigh/Weinmann alloy center-pull with extension levers. Tires are Raleigh 27 × 1¼-inch high-pressure gumwall mounted on chrome-plated steel rims of the same size. Extras include brazed-on cable eyes, guides, and down-tube stops. Frame sizes range from 19¾ to 25 inches. The weight is 30 pounds.
Approximate Retail Price: $196.95
Low Price: Not Available

Peugeot U09 Grand Sport 10-Speed

Best Buy

For the money, this is one of Peugeot's best bicycles. It combines quality workmanship with excellent component parts at an affordable price. That kind of combination is genuinely hard to beat. The frame of this ruggedly constructed touring cycle is of Peugeot 103 lightweight tubing, with a chrome fork crown and ends. The handlebar is a "Franco-Italia" alloy racing style by Atax. The saddle is a Peugeot padded racing style. The derailleurs are the Simplex SX41OGT "Peugeot" (rear) and the Simplex SXA22 (front) with Simplex deluxe power stem shifters. The crankset is the highly regarded Stronglight "99" alloy, cotterless, 40 × 52-tooth with chainguard. The freewheel is the Normany 5-speed, 14 × 28-teeth. The chain is a Sedis 4D. Pedals are by Lyotard 136 rattrap with reflectors. Hubs are Normandy alloy, high-flange with quick-release front. The brakes are the impressive Weinmann 610 alloy center-pull, with 181 quick-release racing levers and marked, "Peugeot." The tires are Michelin 27 × 1¼-inch high-pressure Chevron 50 gumwall, 90 PSI, mounted on Rigida 27 × 1¼-inch Chrolux rims. Extras include spoke protectors, cloth handlebar tape, and wide-angle reflectors. Frame sizes range from 21 to 26 inches. This bicycle would be a good buy at more than its cost; as it stands now, Consumer Guide® commends it as a best buy.
Approximate Retail Price: $235.00
Low Price: $209.96

Peugeot U08 Sport 10-Speed

This model from Peugeot's lineup is very similar to the Grand Sport in appearance and construction. The minor differences (in weight, for example) may make it an excellent buy for the bargain-conscious cyclist. It features a Peugeot 103 lightweight tubing frame with a painted fork. The handlebar is the Atax "Course" racing style. The derailleurs are Simplex SX41OGT "Peugeot" (rear) and Simplex

SXA22 (front) with Simplex deluxe power stem shifters. The crankset is Solida 40 × 52-tooth alloy with chainguard—heavier and less durable than the all-alloy Stronglight crankset on the Grand Sport. The pedals are Lyotard 136 rattrap with safety reflectors. The hubs are Normandy high-flange alloy. The brakes are Weinmann 610 alloy center-pull, with 181 quick-release racing levers and extension levers, marked "Peugeot." The tires are Michelin 27 × 1¼-inch high-pressure Chevron 50 gumwall, 90 PSI, mounted on Rigida 27 × 1¼-inch Chrolux rims. Extras include spoke protectors and wide-angle reflectors. Frame sizes range from 19 to 26 inches.

Approximate Retail Price: $220.00
Low Price: $198.00

Peugeot U010 Course 12-Speed

As a fine, lightweight touring bicycle or a young racer's first competition model cycle, the U010 Course fills the bill. It has a Peugeot 103 lightweight tube frame with chrome fork and ends and an Atax "Franco-Italia" polished alloy handlebar. The stem is of polished Atax PSC96 alloy. The derailleurs are Simplex SX41OGT "Peugeot" (rear) and Simplex SXA22 (front) with Simplex Criterium D/T shifters. The crankset is Stronglight 104 alloy, cotterless, with 40 × 52-tooth chainwheels. The freewheel is the Maillard "Atom" 6-speed, 13-15-17-20-24-28-teeth. The saddle is a Gallet "suede" racing style with an alloy seat post. The hubs are Normandy "Sport" alloy high-flange with quick-release. The brakes are Mafac "Racer" alloy center-pull style with drilled racing levers and full-cover hoods. The chain is a Sedisport 4DCI. The tires are Michelin 27 × 1 (25-360) inch "Bib-Sport 25" gumwall 90 PSI, mounted on Rigida 1622 alloy clincher rims, 27 × 1¼-inch—a lightweight and sturdy combination. Extras include spoke protectors, cloth handlebar tape, and wide-angle reflectors. Frame sizes range from 21 to 26 inches.

Approximate Retail Price: $279.00
Low Price: Not Available

Peugeot PXN1OLE Super Competition

This is Peugeot's top-of-the-line stock racing cycle. It's extremely lightweight, yet durable enough to last through many seasons of racing. It's also a popular bicycle for serious, long-distance tourists. It features a hand-built frame of Reynolds 531 butted tubing, using Nervex lugs and Simplex forged rear drop-outs, with a Reynolds 531 butted fork and full chrome, brazed-on cage fittings. The handlebar is the Atax "Franco-Italia" polished alloy. The stem is the Atax "Peugeot" Professional. The derailleurs are Simplex SX41OTSP "Peugeot" (rear) and Simplex SJA 102 (front) with Simplex SLJ retro-friction alloy shifters. The crankset is the Stronglight "106" alloy cotterless, 42 × 52-teeth. This crankset, by the way, is Stronglight's latest and best yet—both lightweight and reliable. The hubs are Maillard 700 "Peugeot Trophy" alloy, low-flange and polished. The pedals are Atom 600 alloy, black finish with safety reflectors. The saddle is an Ideale 2001 leather racing-style, with an SR Laprade alloy seat post. The brakes are Mafac "LS2" alloy side-pull, with drilled racing levers, full-cover hoods, and quick-release. The tires are Michelin Bib 20 TS foldable, 90 PSI, mounted on Mavic Module E, 700C alloy clincher rims. Extras include spoke protectors, toe clips and straps, cloth handlebar tape, and wide-angle reflectors. Frame sizes range from 20 to 25 inches.

Approximate Retail Price: $599.00
Low Price: Not Available

Peugeot PH8 10-Speed

This is one of Peugeot's new 10-speeds for 1980, built with many of the quality components and construction techniques that have made Peugeot a favored cycle with tourists around the world. The PH8 features a Peugeot 103 lightweight tubing frame and fork, and an Atax PSC96 alloy stem. The handlebar is the Atax "Course" racing style. The derailleurs are Simplex SOO1T (rear), Simplex SA02 (front), with Simplex stem shift levers. The crankset is Nervar 40 × 52-teeth steel, with a chainguard. The hubs are Maillard "Atom" low flange alloy side pull, racing levers with extension levers. The tires are Michelin 27 × 1¼ Chevron 50, 90 PSI, mounted on Rigida 27 × 1¼ Superchromix rims. Extras include

Peugeot's PH8

Huffy's Santa Fe

Huffy's Le Grande

attractive. Reflective rattrap pedals are offered. The saddle is a Huffy custom racing style. Tires are 27 × 1¼-inch high-pressure gumwall. Rims are chrome-plated steel. There are also safety reflectors and steel chainguard. Frame sizes range from 19 to 23 inches. The weight is approximately 36 pounds. Requires partial assembly.
Approximate Retail Price: $110.95
Low Price: $99.99

Huffy LeGrande 12-Speed

Another product of exceptional and innovative graphic appeal, this attractive-looking model bicycle has an unlugged straight-gauge brazed tubular steel frame with brazed-on cable guides. The handlebar is Maes bend with new, thick, durable cushioned grips; the bar is made of steel. The derailleur is a Shimano, front and rear, and shifting is via Huffy's new 12-speed gearing system and stem-mounted shifters. The brakes are Araya center-pull caliper with dual position levers. The crankset is one-piece steel. The hubs are steel. Reflective rattrap pedals are offered. The saddle is Huffy's new "Double Comfort" racing style. Tires are 27 × 1¼-inch high-pressure gumwall mounted on chrome-plated steel rims. There are safety reflectors and chain-guard, as well as a Huffy custom vinyl racing saddle. Frame sizes range from 19 to 23 inches. The weight is approximately 35 pounds. Requires partial assembly.
Approximate Retail Price: $125.41
Low Price: $113.95

Huffy Avanti 10-Speed

This is one of Huffy's top-of-the-line models, featuring a sturdy, lugged frame and several lightweight alloy components. The lugged frame is brazed tubular steel construction with brazed-on cable guides. The seat post and stem are steel. The handlebar is steel, Maes bend type with black cotton tape. The saddle is Huffy's new "Double Comfort" racing style. The derailleur is by Shimano and features dual stem-mounted shifters. Gearing is 38 to

spoke protector and wide-angle reflectors. Frame sizes range from 21 to 24 inches.
Approximate Retail Price: $184.00
Low Price: Not Available

Huffy Santa Fe 10-Speed

This model is one of the most untraditionally attractive in Huffy's line. The manufacturer is a leader in the field using color, design, and graphics to help sell bicycles. As such, Huffy cycles appeal greatly to the younger cycling set. The Santa Fe features a brazed steel tube frame of unlugged construction. Handlebars are Maes drop style of steel. The seat is vinyl on a steel post. The derailleur is Dia-Compe with stem-mount shift levers; Huffy calls it the "Positron" derailleur gearing system with numbered gears. Gearing range is 38 to 100. The brakes are dual caliper side-pull style with dual position levers. The hubs are steel and either Excel or Union (front) and Shimano (rear) large-flange. There's a one-piece steel crankset. The Maes bend grips are thick, durable, and molded vinyl, perforated and

100. The crankset is a three-piece alloy of cotterless construction. The hubs are steel, large-flange. Brakes are Shimano alloy center-pull caliper with dual position brake levers. The tires are 27 × 1¼-inch high-pressure gumwall mounted on 27 × 1¼-inch all-alloy, lightweight rims. Frame size is 23 inches. The weight is approximately 30 pounds, heavy by comparison to most other lightweight models reviewed in this book, but lighter by far than any other of Huffy's models, due to the partial use of alloy components. Requires partial assembly.
Approximate Retail Price: $135.41
Low Price: $123.96

Huffy Strider 10-Speed

Getting back to basics symbolizes this model in the manufacturer's line. It features a brazed, unlugged steel tube frame with steel seat post and stem and plastic strap-type, cable guides, which, according to Huffy, are as durable as—or more so than—steel guides. Still, we'd suggest that, if you buy this model, you pick up a few replacement guides in case the originals snap. The handlebar is steel, Maes-type drop style, and the saddle is Huffy's custom vinyl racing style. The derailleur is by Shimano and features stem-mounted shifters. Gearing is 36 to 97. The crankset is one-piece steel with steel chainguard. The hubs are steel, small-flange. Brakes are dual caliper. The tires are 26 × 1⅜-inch blackwall mounted on steel rims. Pedals are steel with safety reflectors. Frame sizes range from 19 to 21 inches. The weight is approximately 38 pounds. Requires partial assembly.
Approximate Retail Price: $99.00
Low Price: $89.95

Ross Gran Tour 10-Speed

Mention the name, Ross, and most knowledgeable cyclists think of quality and value. While Ross lightweight touring bicycles aren't as light as, say, Schwinn, Motobecane, or Peugeot, Ross cycles boast such construction techniques as lugged frames, welded

Huffy's Avanti

Huffy's Strider

cable stops, positive-action kickstands, and five-step paint finish—all of which adds up to durability and long-lasting value. The Ross Gran Tour is an example. It has a fully lugged, tempered steel frame with welded cable stops and double-tapered rear stays and brazed rear drop outs. It also features a Continental-style headset and bottom bracket assembly. The fork is high-tensile steel (which adds weight, but is nonetheless

very sturdy) with chrome tips and crown cover. The handlebar is randonneur style drop, and the stem is lightweight alloy featuring Allen key expander bolt. The derailleur is Ross-approved alloy construction, and shifters are alloy ratchet stem-mounted. The crankset is an alloy, three-piece cotterless construction with alloy 5-pin, 40 to 52-tooth double chainwheel. Hubs are Ross-approved alloy, large-flange with quick release.

Ross' Gran Tour

Ross' Eurosport

Ross' Super Gran Tour

Brakes are Ross-approved alloy center-pull (men's style) and side-pull (ladies' style) with alloy quick-release hooded levers and safety levers. Tires are 27 × 1⅛-inch, high-pressure, low-resistance gumwall mounted on Ross-built double nickel chrome-plated tubular steel rims. Pedals are weighted, reflectorized ball-bearing construction with rattrap. Frame sizes range from 19 to 25 inches.
Approximate Retail Price: $167.95
Low Price: $151.45

Ross Eurosport 10-Speed

This classical style bicycle is a good buy, with its heavy but rugged fully lugged and tempered steel tubular frame featuring welded cable stops, double-tapered rear stays, and brazed rear drop outs. The fork is tubular tempered steel with chrome tips and crown clover. The handlebar is Nicholson style drop with alloy extended stem. The saddle is a leather-look racing style. The derailleur is the Ross-approved front and rear system with alloy ratchet stem shifter and 14 to 28-tooth rear cluster. The crankset is Shimano's front freewheeling system with one-piece, hot-formed, drop-forged crank and 39 to 52-tooth double chainwheel. The hubs are Ross-approved small-flange. Brakes are Ross-approved alloy side-pull model calipers with alloy hooded levers and safety levers. Tires are 27 × 1¼ gumwall, somewhat more sluggish and prone to rolling resistance than high-pressure "touring"-style tires. Rims are Ross-built double nickel chrome-plated tubulars. Pedals are rattrap reflectorized ball-bearing construction. Frame sizes range from 19-inch (ladies') to 21-inch (men's).
Approximate Retail Price: $179.95
Low Price: $163.95

Ross Super Gran Tour 10-Speed

Quality construction and many excellent component parts distinguish this—Ross' top-of-the-line touring bicycle. Though heavier

than many other touring bikes in its class, this model is attractively built and a good value. The Super Gran Tour features a fully lugged, tempered-steel tubular frame with welded cable stops, double-tapered rear stays, and brazed rear drop outs. There's a Continental-style headset and bottom bracket assembly. The fork is high-tensile, somewhat heavy steel, with eyelet ends, chrome tips, and crown cover, as well as Continental-style fork fittings. The handlebar is alloy randonneur-style with alloy extended stem featuring Allen key expander bolt. The derailleur is Shimano's 600 EX, front and rear, made of lightweight alloy with downtube shifters and gold 14 to 28-tooth rear cluster. The crankset is alloy three-piece cotterless construction with alloy, 5-pin, 42 to 52-tooth double chainwheel featuring replaceable sprockets. The hubs are Ross-approved large-flange, quick-release ball bearing type, front and rear. Brakes are Shimano 600 alloy side-pull style with quick release, tire guides, and drilled-out hooded levers and gum rubber hand cushions. Tires are low rolling resistance high-pressure, 27 × 1⅛-inch gumwall mounted on Ross-built alloy rims. Pedals are weighted, reflectorized, ball-bearing type with rattrap, toe clips, and straps. Extras include engraved black anodized headset and alloy fluted seat pillar.
Approximate Retail Price: $239.95
Low Price: Not Available

Murray's Citation

Murray's Phoenix

Murray Citation 10-Speed

This is an attractive bicycle with some fine features in a comparatively low-cost machine. In addition, it boasts Murray's exclusive hydro-electro finish, renowned for its high gloss protection and eye-catching graphic appeal. The Citation has a frame of tubular lugged steel with tubular steel randonneur-style handlebar and vinyl covering. The saddle is a flo-mold vinyl corduroy look by Troxle. The derailleur is Shimano Sun Tour front and rear with stem-mounted 10-speed shifters. The crankset is three-piece steel,

somewhat heavier (reflected in the overall weight of this model) than alloy sets. Hubs, too, are steel, small-flange. Brakes are the very responsive Dia-Compe center-pull, dual-position caliper of lightweight alloy. Tires are Dae Yung high-pressure tanwall, 27 × 1¼ inches. The front fork is of tubular steel with chrome-plated tips for a nice looking accent. Pedals are rattrap ball-bearing. Also features welded cable guides. Frame sizes range from 19 to 25 inches. Weight is a hefty 38 pounds.
Approximate Retail Price: $135.95
Low Price: $124.95

Murray Phoenix 10-Speed

This model, one of the more popular in Murray's line of derailleur-equipped bicycles, is a very attractive machine with some reasonably impressive components for the money. It's offered in two different frame construction types, however, so it pays to beware of which you're purchasing. Phoenix model number 0-7072 features a tubular steel lugged frame for greatest strength. Phoenix models 0-6472 and 0-6573, though, have frames of tubular butted (not lugged) steel—

Murray's Outrage

AMF's Black Gold Deluxe Racer

less expensive but less apt to hold up to the rigors of hard cycling. Beyond that, the specifications are nearly identical. The handlebar is of tubular steel, drop-style randonneur with molded plastic covering that's neither as comfortable nor as cool as cotton tape. The derailleur is Shimano's Positron-3 10-speed with stem-mounted shifters. The saddle is a Troxle racing style vinyl. The crankset is single-piece steel. Brakes are Araya center-pull, dual-position steel caliper. Hubs are small-flange steel. Tires are Dae Yung 27 × 1¼-inch tanwall mounted on tubular steel, chrome-plated rims. Frame sizes range from 19 to 25 inches.
Approximate Retail Price: $140.00
Low Price: $118.87

Murray Outrage 12-Speed

Responding to the demands of the younger cycling crowd, this model boasts the popular 12-speed derailleur system and what Murray calls OUTRAGEous Graphics—

hardly an overstatement. As the catalog describes, the Outrage is "Extravagant. Aflame with Outrageous Colors. Painted in Outrageous Silver Mist with touches of Black Cherry, Flamboyant Midnight Blue or Flamboyant Red." As if that weren't enough, there are yellow and orange stripe highlights on the frame, fork, and saddle. The Outrage features a frame of tubular butted steel with a tubular steel handlebar of the randonneur drop style, and a tubular fork with chrome-tip plating. The saddle is vinyl by Troxle. There is also vinyl molded covering on the handlebar. The derailleur is Shimano's Positron-3 12-speed with stem-mounted shifters. The crankset is single-piece steel. The hubs are small-flange steel. The brakes are Araya steel-construction side-pull dual-position—not the most efficient imaginable. The tires are the somewhat oversized 26 × 1⅜-inch blackwall mounted on 26 × 1⅜-inch rims. Frame sizes range from 19 to 22 inches. The weight is approximately 39 pounds, heavy for a bike this size; a good, inexpensive, knock-around first bike, but hardly suitable for touring. Partial assembly is required.
Approximate Retail Price: $110.00
Low Price: $87.00

AMF Roadmaster Black Gold 10-Speed

This manufacturer, who distributes its bicycles through a variety of chain, discount, and specialty goods stores, knows the value of attractive design and attention to detailing in capturing a share of the derailleur-dollar. While serious tourists eschew the construction techniques and the components used in AMF machines, these multi-speed bikes are, in fact, suitably built for average road use—if a bit on the heavy side. The Black Gold, for instance, features a butted steel tubing, electric-welded frame with chrome-plated Maesbend steel handlebar with suede-feel tape. The saddle is AMF-approved "stitch grained" (which means vinyl made to look like leather) racing style. Brakes are

AMF's Decathalon

AMF's Scorcher

AMF-approved steel center-pull, front and rear, with dual position levers. The derailleur is the best feature of ths bike—by Shimano—the Positron system with the Quick-Shift single lever shifter developed by AMF; it lets the rider pre-select gears (from 1 to 10), read the numeral corresponding to the gear the bike is in, and in general simplifies the act of shifting. Hubs are small-flange steel, as is the one-piece crank. Pedals are steel rattrap. Tires are 27 × 1¼-inch gumwall mounted on the same size steel rims. The frame size is 23 inches. Partial assembly is required.

Approximate Retail Price: $129.88
Low Price: $117.95

AMF Roadmaster Decathalon 10-Speed

Similar in construction to the Black Gold, but in smaller frame and wheel sizes to appeal to younger riders. The frame is butted steel tube, electric-weld construction. Handlebar is Maes bend with chrome-plating and suede-feel tape. Saddle is vinyl racing style. Derailleur is Shimano's Positron with AMF's Quick-Shift SLS (single-lever shifting) system. The crankset is single-piece steel. Hubs are small-flange steel front and rear. Brakes are AMF-approved steel side-pull on girl's models, a definite disadvantage, as the brakes we tested were difficult to adjust in order to achieve uniform tension on all brake pads. Brakes

on boy's models are center pull. Tires are 26 × 1⅜ inch gumwall mounted on steel rims of the same size. In 21 (men's) and 19-inch sizes. Partial assembly is required.

Approximate Retail Price: $129.88
Low Price: $117.95

AMF Roadmaster Pursuit 12-Speed

This machine, the only 12-speed cycle in AMF's lineup, is a popular street machine especially with young riders. It features a sporty touring look, although its typical AMF heavy weight makes it a better around-town bike. The frame, for instance, is of butted tubular steel, electrically welded, with a chrome-plated Maes-bend handlebar with washable black suede-feel tape. The fork is steel, and the derailleur is Shimano Positron with Positron III stem-mounted shifters. The crankset consists of single-piece steel construction. Front hub is small-flange steel; the rear is Shimano's Uni-Balance. The pedals are rat trap style. The tires are 27 × 1¼-inch gumwall mounted on steel, chrome-plated rims. The frame size is 23 inches. Partial assembly is required.

Approximate Retail Price: $111.88
Low Price: $100.95

AMF Roadmaster Scorcher 10-Speed

This is a bare-bones model 10-speed bicycle with few fancy or exceptionally attractive com-

ponents. But, then, in this price range, one shouldn't expect a Motobecane. The Scorcher's frame is butted tubular steel, electrically welded, with chrome-plated Maes bend steel handlebar and vinylized tape. The derailleur is Excel, front and rear, with a gearing ratio of 36 to 97. The saddle is vinyl racing style. Brakes are hooded-lever steel side-pull caliper, front and rear. Tires are 26 × 1⅜ inches mounted on chrome-plated steel rims. This is a heavy machine for its size, which is 21 inches (men's) and 19 inches (ladies'). Partial assembly is required.

Approximate Retail Price: $89.98
Low Price: $79.95

ONE-, TWO-, AND THREE-SPEED BICYCLES

Ross Compact Three-Speed

This model bicycle, a popular seller in the Ross line, features tempered steel tubular frame with welded cable stops and tubular tempered-steel fork with chrome crown cover. The handlebar is Northroad style (tourist), between standard upright and traditional drop-bar racing. The gears are Shimano three-speed hub with trigger control. (Also available in a model featuring Shimano trimatic three-speed with coaster brake.) The crankset is a single-piece, hot-formed, drop-forged crank with a 48-tooth front

Ross' Compact

Huffy's Timberline

Peugeot's VX40 and VX45

sprocket. Hubs are Ross-approved ball-bearing style. The brakes are Ross-approved alloy side-pull caliper, front and rear. (Also available with Ross-approved coaster brake). Pedals are reflectorized ball bearing construction. Tires are 26 × 1⅜-inch gumwall on 3-speed and trimatic models; 26 × 1.75-inch blackwall on coaster-brake models. Rims are Ross-built double nickel chrome-plated tubular steel. Extras include ten-inch seat post for maximum adjustment range and safety cushion. The frame size is 17½ inches.
Approximate Retail Price: $119.95
Low Price: $108.95

Huffy Timberline Three-Speed

This somewhat heavy, sturdily constructed bicycle features a butted tubular steel construction frame with plastic cable straps. Handlebar is upright style of tubular steel. Gears consist of three-speed gearing system with trigger control shifter. The brakes are Huffy-approved dual caliper. The saddle is mattress-style with spring construction of leather-like vinyl. The pedals are safety reflectorized ball-bearing construction. The tires are 26 × 1⅜-inch blackwall mounted on chrome-plated steel rims. Extras include matching front-and-rear fenders and chain guard. The frame size is 21 inches. Requires partial assembly.
Approximate Retail Price: $89.90
Low Price: $79.95

Peugeot VX40 Deluxe Men's 3-Speed and VX45 Deluxe Ladies' 3-Speed

The VX40 and VX45 deluxe men's and ladies' 3-speed touring bicycles, new members of the Peugeot line for 1980, provide the casual cyclist with Peugeot quality and comfort. The VX40 and VX45 feature Peugeot lightweight tubing frames and forks, fully lugged. The handlebar is the Atax "Brighton" touring style, with grips included on the ladies' model. The crankset is of "Peugeot" SR alloy, 46T, with a full-cover deluxe chainguard. The

Schwinn's Collegiate Tourist

Murray's Escort

hubs are Sturmey Archer AW 3-speed rear, 19T, with a trigger shift, and Maillard "Atom" alloy front. The brakes are the Mafac "Racer" alloy center-pull style with alloy touring levers on the men's model, and Weinmann 734 alloy side-pull style with alloy touring levers on the ladies' model. The tires are Michelin "Sport" 700 × 35C, mounted on Rigida Chrolux 700C rims. The many extras include full chrome fenders (with rear skirt guard on the ladies' model), rear luggage carrier, Soubitez No. 3 generator light set, kickstand, pump, bell, and wide-angle reflectors. The men's bicycle is available in frame sizes from 21 to 24 inches, and the ladies' in 21 to 23 inch frame sizes.
Approximate Retail Price: $289.00
Low Price: Not Available

Schwinn Collegiate Tourist Three-Speed

Best Buy

This is a ruggedly constructed bicycle in the traditional Schwinn mold. It's a good value in long-lasting riding comfort and satisfaction. It features a Schwinn electro-forged frame of 16-gauge 1010 carbon steel tubing with built-in kickstand housing. The fork is Schwinn-built forged steel. The handlebar is Schwinn steel chrome-plated, touring (upright) style. The saddle is a mattress-style (with springs) Mesinger SI-5, exclusively designed for Schwinn. The crankset is Schwinn's one-piece chrome-plated forged-steel

crank with 46-tooth chainwheel. The hub is three-speed. There's a Sturmey-Archer handlebar trigger control. The brakes are Schwinn-approved side-pull caliper (front and rear). The pedals are Schwinn-approved Union rubber block. The tires are Schwinn Sports Touring 26 × 1¼-inch gumwall mounted on Schwinn-approved tubular steel, chrome-plated 26 × 1¼-inch Endrick EA-1 rims. Frame sizes range from 17 to 24 inches. Weight is approximately 39 pounds, with built-in kickstand. Because of the quality construction and assembly, this bicycle is a Consumer Guide® best buy.
Approximate Retail Price: $151.95
Low Price: Not Available

Murray Escort Three-Speed

This no-frills, no-nonsense machine features a butted tubular steel frame and upright tourist handlebars. The saddle is a quilt-design foam-filled mattress, spring-style. The gearing is Shimano's Trimatic hub with coaster brake. The Trimatic shifter can be operated by the thumb without moving your hand. The front hub is small-flange steel. The tires are Dae Yung 26 × 1⅜-inch tanwall mounted on tubular steel rims of the same size. The pedals are Wald ball-bearing. Extras include steel fenders and chainguard. Partial assembly is required.
Approximate Retail Price: $95.00
Low Price: $84.24

Murray Nassau Single-Speed

What can you say about a proven best seller that's as simple to operate as its lines are to look at? The Nassau is a single-speed coaster-brake model bicycle with a heavy-duty tubular steel frame-and-fork construction. The handle-bar is tourist style of chrome-plated tubular steel. The saddle is a leather-look mattress style with spring cushioning. There are steel fenders front and rear and a full-length chainguard. The pedals are ball bearing with safety reflectors. The tires are Dae Yung 16 × 1⅜-inch blackwall mounted on chrome-plated tubular steel rims. Frame size is 22 inches. Partial assembly is required.
Approximate Retail Price: $78.95
Low Price: $70.00

Murray Monterey Two-Speed Automatic

It was bound to happen. Given enough time and reason, someone was bound to introduce an auto-shifting bicycle. The Monterey Magna Two-Speed Automatic is it. It's a real balloon-tire bike promoted by Murray as ideal for "beach, park, or bike path." That's true, of course, as long as the trip isn't too long. Even with the exclusive two-speed auto shifter, pedaling this machine requires a bit of dedication over the long haul. It's built of tubular steel frame construction with extra reinforcing bars on the men's style model. The

Murray's Nassau

Murray's Monteray

handlebar is upright and equipped with vinyl grips. The seat is spring mattress style, of vinyl, mounted on a chrome-plated tubular steel post. The rear hub is a Sachs Magna Two-Speed Automatic that automatically shifts to a higher gear as cycling speed increases, then shifts down to the lower gear as speed decreases. While this type of hub is a real advantage on a heavyweight bike, it's surprising Murray doesn't offer it, too, on its lighter "touring" single-speed Nassau. The Monterey's tires are giant 26 × 2⅛-inch Carlisle wide whitewall mounted on heavy-duty chrome-plated steel rims. There's a full-length chainguard and extra wide steel fender over each wheel. A coaster brake rounds out the package. Also available in single-speed model. Partial assembly is required.
Approximate Retail Price: $98.95
Low Price: $90.00

AMF Courier Single Speed

This AMF single-speed model is available in both men's and ladies' style frames. The diamond frame is made of heavy butted tubular steel and has a chromed steel "European"-style touring handlebar. This, along with the spring touring-style saddle make pedaling over any but the smoothest, shortest terrain, a tough job. There is a full-length chainguard and the pedals are reflectorized, black rubber. The tires are 26 × 1⅜-inch blackwalls

mounted on heavy steel rims. Partial assembly is required.
Approximate Retail Price: $90.00
Low Price: $81.00

TANDEM BICYCLES

Schwinn Twinn Sport Tandem 10-Speed **Best Buy**

Bicycles built for two have changed since the days when Daisy looked so neat upon the seat. New construction, lighter materials, and a 10-speed derailleur have updated this model into an easy handling, durable and fun bicycle for touring the countryside or riding around the block. The frame is a 22-inch front and 20-inch rear, of partially hand-brazed carbon steel construction. Handlebars are drop-style in front and a cross between drop-style and upright in the rear called "All-

Rounder" made of chrome-plated steel. The saddles are Schwinn Comfort Form racing style. The crankset is made of alloy, three-piece cotterless construction for light weight and long wear. The derailleur is the GT510 (rear) and the GT290 (front) with stem-mounted shifters in front. The brakes are internal expander type, both rear and front. The tires are Schwinn Puff gumwall, 27 × 1¼-inches, on chrome-plated steel rims of the same size. The approximate weight is 52 pounds. At a price indicative of a bicycle-built-for-one, this tandem is a Consumer Guide® best buy.
Approximate Retail Price: $288.95
Low Price: Not Available

Motobecane Inter Club Tandem 10-Speed

Good pulling power on uphill grades and a lightweight frame

Schwinn's Twinn Sport

Motobecane's Inter Club

combine to make this an easy cycling machine that results in fun. It's a far cry from the days when a tandem bike meant two singles welded together. This sleek, stylish model features a lightweight 2040 high resiliency tube construction frame with Bardon tandem headset and Motobecane racing bend bar (front) and dropped-type with soft sleeves (rear). The stems, front and rear, are lightweight Sakae alloy with recessed bolts. Brakes are center-pull Maillard. The derailleur is the Sun Tour Compe V (front) and the Sun Tour V-GT Luxe (rear) with stem-mounted shifters. The rear cluster is five-speed, either Maillard or Maeda, with 24 to 32 teeth and finished in black. The chain is a black-finish Sedis, and the crankset is TA special tandem, 40 to 52-tooth double chainwheel with chain guard. The pedals are the Lyotard 136R chrome-plated with safety reflectors. The hubs are Atom low-flange (front) and Maillard drum brake (rear). The saddles are the comfortable padded Touring Record E. The bicycle is equipped with CPSC approved safety reflectors. Tires are 27 × 1¼-inch Motobecane-Hutchinson high-pressure gumwall

mounted on 27 × 1¼-inch Rigida chrome-plated rims with spoke protectors. The frame size is 22 inches (front) and 20¾ inches (rear). The weight is approximately 45½ pounds, making this one of the lightest tandems currently in production.
Approximate Retail Price: $639.00
Low Price: Not Available

CHILDREN'S, HI-RISE, AND MOTO-CROSS BICYCLES

Schwinn Competition Scrambler SX-2000 BMX Best Buy

Moto-cross competitive riding requires a bicycle that can stand up to stress from sharp turns, quick acceleration and plenty of jumps. The heart of this new moto-cross bicycle is designed to do just that. It's a frame featuring a unique ovular tubing of chrome moly-bdenum steel throughout, hand-brazed and butted with thicker tube-end walls to take high stress and strain. The increased distance between the top and bottom joints results in increased leverage and a reduction of the load on the tubes.

This model also features a tubular chrome molybdenum competition fork, anodized Sun Tour double clamp stem, rear caliper brakes, quick-change alloy sprocket, and a Troxel BMX saddle of quality construction. The approximate weight is 28 pounds. Despite the rather high price, the durable ovular frame and quality components throughout are well worth the money, making this light weight racing machine a Consumer Guide® best buy. In Chrome with Red Trim, Chrome with Blue Trim, or full chrome plate.
Approximate Retail Price: $268.95
Low Price: Not Available

Rampar R-10 BMX Best Buy

In a sport in which seconds often mark the difference between finishing in or out of the gold, the R-10 appears to be too heavy to be taken as a serious competitor. Still, its heavy-duty construction and obvious value for the money have made it one of Rampar's best-selling BMX bicycles and one of America's finest street bikes. Its frame, of MIG-welded carbon steel, is 12 inches in size, with steel, box design handlebars in a flat-black enamel finish. The brakes are Sun

Schwinn's Competition Scrambler SX-2000 BMX

Schwinn's SX 500 BMX

Schwinn's SX 100 BMX

Tour coaster style for virtually no-maintenance wear. The crankset is Sugino's forged steel, one-piece with 40-tooth chainwheel. The tires are 20 × 2.125-inch MX Knobby mounted on chrome-plated steel rims of the same size. The saddle is Rampar's Hi-Tail, padded, of quilted vinyl. The hubs are chrome-plated, low-flange steel. There's also a padded cross brace for rider safety. The approximate weight is 35 pounds. Despite its hefty weight, the quality components and construction at a reasonable cost make this bicycle a Consumer Guide® best buy. In Flamboyant Copper, Chinese Red, Chinese Blue, Royal Blue, or All Chrome.
Approximate Retail Price: $164.95
Low Price: Not Available

Schwinn SX 500 BMX

This high-quality bicycle features several exclusive Schwinn components and sensible, safe construction. It's most popular as a street bike, with its exclusive Schwinn Magalloy metal alloy wheels on an entirely new flash-welded, carbon steel BMX-style frame. It's gusset reinforced to take the bumps and jumps. There's also a new competition saddle and steel hubs with coaster brake rear. A handlebar brace and BMX-style grips add to overall performance and rider control. The pedals are ball-bearing construction. The wheels are new mag-style. The fork is of chrome-plated steel of tubular construction. The tires are Knobby style on Magalloy metal rims. The approximate weight is 32 pounds. In paint finish, or all chrome.
Approximate Retail Price: $181.95
Low Price: Not Available

Schwinn SX 100 BMX

This fine street bike features the same popular BMX styling and many of the same construction techniques and component parts of the SX 500. It features Schwinn flash-welded carbon steel frame with gusset reinforcement where needed, to produce the strongest frame of its type. The new mag wheels are star-design, made with

84

glass fiber reinforced nylon. The saddle is a newly designed quilted competition style. There's also a cross-braced handlebar of tubular steel in hi-rise style. The brakes are coaster style. The fork is chrome-plated steel of tubular construction. The tires are Knobby style on one-piece mag rims. The approximate weight is 32 pounds. In Frosty Silver, Spicy Chestnut, Cardinal Red, or all chrome.
Approximate Retail Price: $196.95
Low Price: Not Available

Schwinn Scrambler 36-36 Series

This bicycle, although somewhat heavy for BMX competition, offers traditional BMX rugged construction and many of the advanced features sought in a high-performance racing or street bike. The frame is Schwinn's carbon steel tube construction, reinforced with gusset for extra strength. There's a freewheeling rear wheel with caliper brakes or coaster brakes. The fork is of chrome-plated steel. The saddle is Schwinn's quilted competition style. The tires are Knobby, mounted on steel tubular rims with 36 spokes in each wheel to add strength at minimum weight to make this machine a favorite on tracks and on the streets all over the country. The weight is approximately 33 pounds. In Cardinal Red, Sky Blue, or all chrome.
Approximate Retail Price: $176.95
Low Price: Not Available

Schwinn Phantom Scrambler

If you're looking for a way to get in on all the fun and excitement of BMX action without having to make a large initial investment, you'll be pleased with this bike. It's a good value in a solidly built street and racing machine. It features a Schwinn forged steel fork and tubular steel butted frame. The saddle is the new Schwinn competition style. There's an easy-to-use and hard to abuse coaster brake. The handlebar is Schwinn's popular hi-rise style with safety grips and brace bar. The pedals are ball-bearing with rubber. The tires are Schwinn Scrambler Knobby, 20

Schwinn's Scrambler 36-36

Schwinn's Phantom Scrambler

× 2.125-inch type, mounted on either nylon Mag star-design or traditional spoked rims. The weight is 33 pounds. In Black Sable, Cardinal Red, Sky Blue, or chrome plated.
Approximate Retail Price: $141.95
Low Price: Not Available

Schwinn Hurricane 5 **Best Buy**

For the child who has always wanted a truly deluxe, fully equipped bike, this is it. It combines the popular styling of BMX with the versatility of a multi-gear derailleur system featuring positive, safe shifting. The frame is Schwinn's exclusive cantilever design of tubular butted steel. The handlebar is hi-rise style with a cross brace for added strength and safety. The five-speed model has a five-speed gear system using the Positron II gear shifting system that makes changing gears a "snap." (This

Schwinn's Hurricane 5

Schwinn's Tornado

semi-hi-rise handlebar. Both the fork and stem are of steel tube construction. The saddle is black padded with sporty brace design. Brakes are coaster type. The tires are 20 × 1¾-inch deep-tread blackwall mounted on steel rims. There's a built-in kickstand, a simulated MX tank, sporty mini-mudguards, a full-length chain-guard, and a big, bold license number plate mounted on the cross brace. The weight is 34 pounds. Available in Black with Golden Yellow Trim.
Approximate Retail Price: $101.95
Low Price: Not Available

Schwinn Bantam

This cycle is excellent for the young, growing family—a good first "pass-along" bike that should last through years and years of hard use. It's a 20-inch model with tubular frame construction featuring a convertible boys'-girls' style changeover feature. By removing the bolts in the top bar, the bike is quickly and easily converted into a "girls'-style" machine (which is the easiest type to learn on for both boys and girls). The saddle is the mattress spring type, and the bars are upright (not high rise), of tubular chrome-plated steel. There's a steel stem with a ball-bearing head set. The Bantam also features coaster brakes, a full-length chainguard, chrome-plated fenders on the front and rear, ball-bearing reflectorized pedals, and spoked wheels. The tires are Schwinn 20 × 1¾-inch nylon cord mounted on chrome-plated tubular steel rims. The weight is 32 pounds. Available in Cardinal Red or Sky Blue.
Approximate Retail Price: $96.95
Low Price: Not Available

Schwinn Sting-Ray Pixie

Just one of Schwinn's popular Sting-Ray-style bikes, this model is a best bet for youngsters to learn with and have fun with. It has a tubular steel frame construction of the mixte style—halfway between traditional boys' and traditional girls' styling—making it a popular

bike is also available as a coaster-brake model.) The saddle is a ribbed-design, MX-style with augmented braces—both big and sporty. The rear tire is Knobby design mounted on a tubular steel rim with 36 spokes (both front and rear). The weight is a hefty 40 pounds, but the handling makes up for it. For children old enough to operate a multi-geared bike, the quality of construction and atten-tion to detailing make this a

Consumer Guide® best buy. In Blue and Silver or Red and Silver combinations.
Approximate Retail Price: $166.95
Low Price: Not Available

Schwinn Tornado

For the young bicyclist who wants the competition look in a street machine, this model is very sporty and built to last. It has a frame of tubular butted steel and an upright,

Schwinn's Bantam

Schwinn's Pixie Sting Ray

bike with youngsters of either sex. The handlebars are chrome-plated steel and upright; and there's a steel stem and ball-bearing head set. The saddle is adjustable Sting-Ray style. There's a built-in kickstand, full-length chainguard, and safety grips. Tires are Superior Schwinn 16 × 1¾-inch pneumatic on steel spoked rims. The weight is 27 pounds. In Sky Blue or Silver Mist.
Approximate Retail Price: $84.95
Low Price: Not Available

Schwinn Convertible Lil' Tiger

This model bike is a fine beginner's cycle—with one possible exception. It features a tubular steel frame with easily removable top bar to appeal to either boys or girls. It's a compact design complete with

Schwinn Cycle Aid training wheels. There are chrome fenders, padded Sting-Ray-style saddle, full-length chainguard, and chrome-plated, semi-hi-rise handlebar. This last feature is definitely a detriment to the cyclist just learning to maintain balance. A youngster is apt to be very unsure of himself—even with the addition of the training wheels—and the semi-hi-rise bar won't add to a feeling of stability. Consider substituting a standard upright handlebar, especially for petite youngsters just learning to ride. The Lil' Tiger also features 12-inch, puncture-proof, semi-pneumatic tires on steel spoked rims. A fixed gear (direct drive) allows forward and backward pedaling for stopping and overall maneuverability (there is no coaster brake). The weight is 25

pounds. Available in Cardinal Red or Sky Blue.
Approximate Retail Price: $71.95
Low Price: Not Available

Huffy Sweet Thunder

This attractive girls'-style bicycle is both durable and stylish and should provide years of comfortable riding pleasure. It features a tubular steel frame with chrome-plated handlebar of Hi-Lift style with safety cross brace and coordinated MX hand grips. The saddle is padded Huffy custom Enduro-style with brace. The pedals are reflectorized for safety. There's a single-speed operation with coaster brake. The fenders are extra wide, lightweight. There's also a full-length chainguard and front number plaque. The tires are 20 × 1¾-inch stagger-

Schwinn's Convertible Lil Tiger

Huffy's Sweet Thunder

Huffy's Bandit

Huffy's Cactus Rose

are also included. The tires are Huffy's 20 × 2.125-inch Monster Trac with deep-digging tractor-cleat side tread and smooth linear center tread mounted on gold-chrome tubular steel rims (spoked). In Gloss Black finish with gold-chrome trim and unique Huffy graphics. Partial assembly is required.
Approximate Retail Price: $99.50
Low Price: $89.99

Huffy Thunder Trail

Built for taking the rough dirt tracks, this model is a popular moto-cross machine that's attractive in its simplicity. Designed to hold up to the rigors of day-to-day use, it's constructed of a hard-tail, tubular frame with a gussetted headtube for added strength. This single-speed coaster brake bike has a hi-rise, MX box-style handlebar with a padded crossbar and MX grips. The pedals are reflectorized, and there is a full-length chainguard. The saddle is Huffy's "Tough Rider" struttless-style. The tires are Huffy's 20 × 2.125-inch stagger block blackwalls. The bike also includes lightweight fenders and a front number plaque.
Approximate Retail Price: $89.00
Low Price: $78.87

Huffy Cactus Rose

This girls'-style hi-rise bike with 20-inch tubular steel butted frame offers chrome-plated handlebar with hand grips and the popular Huffy Custom Polo-style saddle with brace. It has sporty extra-wide, lightweight fenders with custom graphics and a full-length chain-guard for safe pedaling fun. The pedals are reflective. The tires are 20 × 1¾-inch blackwall mounted on tubular chrome-plated steel spoked rims. In Eggshell finish with Firefrost fenders. Partial assembly is required.
Approximate Retail Price: $79.00
Low Price: $70.70

Huffy Mini Pro

The Mini Pro is a popular young-ster's bike in a 16-inch size. It

block Knobby style on chrome-plated steel rims. Available in Lolli-pop (pink-and-white) finish. Partial assembly is required.
Approximate Retail Price: $84.95
Low Price: $69.99

Huffy Bandit

Designed to move fast and attract a lot of attention, this Huffy model is another extremely attractive and durable bike in the Huffy lineup for children. It features a rugged tubu-lar steel frame with extra large, oval top tube and high-lift rear stays

designed for maximum style and strength. This single-speed coaster-brake model has Huffy's Hi-Stridin' handlebar with black octopus grips and crossbar-mounted Air Foil, and stem-mounted simulated fog lamps. The Razor Back lightweight fenders with louvered styling and orange-and-gold graphics add to the over-all appeal of this cycle. There's a full-length chainguard which completely encloses the front sprocket (for 360-degree protec-tion). Reflective pedals and exclu-sive Black Bandit saddle by Huffy

features BMX styling in a size for the youngest bicyclist. The frame is tubular steel with a removable top bar for easy conversion from a girls' to a boys' bike, or for learning purposes. The handlebar is upright with a padded cross brace in true BMX tradition. There's a full-length chainguard and mudguard fenders. This one-speed coaster-brake model comes complete with training wheels. In Arctic White finish with Candy Apple Red Trim. Partial assembly is required.
Approximate Retail Price: $53.10
Low Price: $47.70

Huffy Desperado

This 20-inch hi-rise model is one of the most attractive children's bicycles reviewed. It's also built to take the kind of punishment kids are known to dish out. Its frame is of tubular steel butted construction with chrome-plated tubular steel handlebar and hand grips. The saddle is Huffy Custom Polo-style with brace. Fenders are extra-wide, lightweight style. This is a single-speed, coaster-brake model with full-length chainguard and ball-bearing reflectorized pedals. The tires are 20 × 1¾-inch black-wall mounted on tubular chrome-plated steel rims. In Straw finish with Hot Fudge fenders and brown leather-look saddle. Partial assembly is required.
Approximate Retail Price: $65.40
Low Price: $59.90

Huffy Pro 5 BMX

This is the ultimate bike in Huffy's popular new Pro Thunder line. It's loaded with plenty of good features for the serious track or dirt racer. It's also good-looking enough to be a popular street cycle. It features an "advanced design" Huffy frame and tubular fork with a newly designed rear, hand-brazed drop-out style toe plate. The handlebar is of lightweight alloy in a V-line design. There's also an alloy three-piece crank and an alloy seat post. The brake system is rear caliper (Huffy could improve the stopping efficiency by adding a front caliper)

Huffy's Mini Pro

Huffy's Desperado

side-pull style, and there's a rear freewheel hub. The pillow-block stem is padded, as are the top tube and the cross brace. The saddle is a custom racing-style. The pedals are Huffy Thunderline racing style. There are also octopus handlebar grips and a full-length chainguard for added safety. The tires are 20 × 2.125-inch stagger-block Knobby mounted on alloy wheels. Hubs, too, are lightweight alloy. Available in Gloss Black finish with Gold Alloy trim. Partial assembly is required.
Approximate Retail Price: $93.55
Low Price: $84.00

Rampar R-10 Mite-Y-Mite

This scaled-down version of the R-10 is mighty small with only a 10-inch frame. It has a frame of carbon steel, MIG welded, and a carbon steel front fork with leading axle. The handlebar is of steel, mini-box design, and the stem is of forged steel. The brakes are Sun Tour coaster style, and there's a three-piece forged steel crankset with a 32-tooth chainwheel. The pedals are rubber block, and the hubs on this pint-sized piece of action are

Huffy's Pro Thunder 5 BMX

style MX with MX black grips. The stem is forged single stem, and the hubs are Shimano B-Type coaster brake, 36H × 12G, and steel low-flange front, 36H × 12G. The crank is a quality Sugino one-piece forged CP with 46 teeth for real pulling power. Pedals are black, Chro-molybdenum with safety reflectors. The saddle is a steel-base, quilted vinyl racing type. There's also a hockey-stick type chainguard and rear chain adjustors. The tires are Cheng Shim MX, 20 × 2.125-inch Knobby, mounted on 20 × 2.125-inch colored, dimpled steel rims. The quality, lightweight components and competitive price make this a Consumer Guide® best buy. Available in Red, Yellow, or Blue.
Approximate Retail Price: $129.00
Low Price: Not Available

Ross Pantera

This hi-rise style bicycle is a well-built, comfortable riding street machine complete with the kinds of features that make cycling fun. It has a 20-inch, new, RMX heavy-duty gussetted frame and the new, RMX reinforced tubular steel fork. The handlebar is the hi-rise, RMX black, heavy-duty sport-style with padded crossbar and black forged stem. The crankset is a one-piece, hot forged, 6½-inch black crank with a 44-tooth replaceable sprocket. The brakes are Ross-approved alloy caliper, front and rear. The wheels are Ross-built with two-tone anodized alloy rims and a 14-tooth rear freewheel. The tires are 20 × 2.125-inch gumwall, stud, front and 20 × 1.75-inch gumwall stud, rear.
Approximate Retail Price: $190.00
Low Price: Not Available

Ross Polobike

A popular street bike in either boys' or girls' style frame, this machine has been a proven best seller over the years. It features a frame of tempered steel, tubular construction, with a tubular tempered steel with chrome crown cover fork. The handlebar is hi-rise style with handlebar grips. The crankset is a

Ross' Pantera

low-flange steel with chrome plating. The saddle is Rampar's Hi-Tail of padded, quilted vinyl. The cross brace is padded for safety. The tires are 16 × 2.125-inch MX Knobby mounted on 16 × 1.75-inch chrome-plated steel rims. The weight is 24 pounds. For young cyclists, the quality construction, attention to detail, and competitive price make this a Consumer Guide® best buy. Available in Flamboyant Red or Flamboyant Sky Blue.
Approximate Retail Price: $94.95
Low Price: Not Available

Peugeot CPX-100 Motocross   **Best Buy**

Several years ago, the "big-name" bicycle manufacturers both here and abroad were less than enthusiastic about building BMX machines. Today, of course, that's all changed, as evidenced by Peugeot's fine dirt bike entry in the BMX Sweepstakes. It has a rigid-type frame with head tube and bottom bracket gussets. The fork is HX-400MX, chromed, with forward axle mount. The handlebar is box-

Prices are accurate at time of printing; subject to manufacturer's change.

one-piece, hot-formed, drop-forged crank with a 36-tooth front sprocket. The brakes are Ross-approved coaster style. The pedals are reflectorized ball-bearing construction. There are also chrome-plated steel mudguard fenders and a full-length chain-guard. The saddle is banana-style with brace. The tires are 20 × 1.75-inch, front and rear, mounted on Ross-built double nickel chrome-plated steel rims with Ross-approved ball-bearing hubs. In Scarlet Red, or Peacock Blue (boys'), and Pastel Blue, or Pink (girls').

Approximate Retail Price: $143.95
Low Price: $129.00

Ross Slinger

This 20-inch, hi-rise moto-cross bicycle features a new RMX heavy-duty gussetted frame with the new RMX reinforced tubular steel fork. The handlebar is the RMX black, heavy-duty sport-style, with a crossbar and forged stem. The crankset is a one-piece, hot forged 5½-inch crank, with a 44-tooth sprocket. The brakes are Ross-approved coaster-style. The wheels are Ross-built with steel rims and Ross-approved hubs. The tires on the Slinger are 20 × 2.125-inch Mud stud. Two of the Slinger models, 13-636 and 25-636, include mud guards and a padded crossbar.

Approximate Retail Price: $120.00
Low Price: Not Available

Ross Snapper BMX

This model is Ross' most serious entrant into the BMX Derby. It's a truly competitive machine, designed for speed and durability. The frame on the Snapper is Ross' new MX gussetted and brazed heavy-duty tubular with a tubular chrome-plated steel reinforced MX fork. The handlebar is RMX black, heavy-duty sport style with crossbar and black-forged stem. The crankset is a one-piece, hot-formed, drop-forged 6½-inch black crank with a 44-tooth sprocket. The brakes are Ross-approved coaster style. Pedals are reflectorized for

Ross' Polobike

Ross' Snapper BMX

safety. There's a full-length chain-guard. The tires are 20 × 2.125-inch Mud Stud mounted on heavy duty wheels with 36-105-gauge spokes and high-flange black front hub. It's also available with poly-urethane star-design mag wheels. Available in Peacock Blue or Flat Black.

Approximate Retail Price: $159.95
Low Price: $144.99

Murray BMX 0-5360

These Murray BMX bicycles are built to take it and keep right on going. They're light yet sturdy, with

many of the features that mark the difference between an ordinary street bike and a real BMX racing machine. Murray's 5360 top-of-the-line BMX features a butted tubular steel frame with a functional gusset for added strength on jumps. The new pillow block stem of part alloy, part steel is similarly built to absorb some of the shocks peculiar to BMX racing bikes. There's a rugged 6½-inch crank and a freewheel rear hub. A single rear Araya caliper brake provides for smooth, fast stopping power. The sprocket is a quick-change alloy three-piece construction for lightweight and

Murray's Team BMX Model 05360

Murray's Team BMX Model 05346

durable running. The Murray comfort-formed saddle is color-keyed to the handgrips, top brace, and handlebar pad. It's made of extra lightweight plastic. There's also a rear entry wheel clip for fast on-off of the wheel. Tires are 20-inch tanwall knobby mounted on steel rims with 36 spokes both front and rear. The fork is of heavy-gauge welded steel with chrome plating. The pedals are heavy-duty BMX style. Available in a chrome frame with black accents.
Approximate Retail Price: $133.95
Low Price: Not Available

Murray BMX 0-5346

This popular street and track machine features a tubular steel frame and a BMX handlebar with cross brace. There's a gusseted four-inch head that adapts to custom MX fork assemblies. The saddle is BMX-style padded vinyl. There's a one-piece steel crank and a coaster brake rear hub. The fork is tubular steel. The tires are 20-inch blackwall knobby mounted on Trac-Master mag nylon and polyurethane wheels. The slotted rear wheel clip allows for quick chain adjustments and rear wheel replacement. Extras include a full-length chainguard and top tube, stem, and brace pads. Available in Flamboyant Red with Yellow accessories. Partial assembly is required.
Approximate Retail Price: $108.40
Low Price: Not Available

AMF Roadmaster Hawk

This new competition strength BMX features all Mig welded construction with heavy-duty gussets at stress points, and tough leading-edge tubular MX fork. The handlebar is a "box-bar" MX style with black octopus MX grips. There is a deluxe padded crossbar, fork stem, and top bar. The saddle is a black quilt-top MX racing style. Pedals are reflectorized, and there is a single-speed coaster brake hub. The tires are 20 × 2.125-inch (rear), mounted on AMF's Mag

AMF's Hawk 5 BMX

Force Lester alloy wheels, both strong and attractive.

Approximate Retail Price: $85.95
Low Price: $73.99

AMF Roadmaster Avenger 360 BMX

This moto-cross-style machine is an attractive and durable, if somewhat awkward handling, bike that features butted steel tube frame with top bar and heavy-duty gussets at stress points. The fork is AMF's exclusive alloy "Rally" style. The handlebar is MX-style and doesn't appear to be as sturdy as traditional tubular steel constructions. There is, however, a cross brace, though it and the top tube are unpadded—a definite disadvantage to the young BMX racer. The 20 × 2.125-inch Knobby wrap-around tires are mounted on AMF's exclusive "Mag Force" wheels, built by the Lester Wheel Company, the largest supplier of motorcycle aftermarket wheels of heat-treated, cast aluminum alloy—very impressive for rugged on-track use.

Approximate Retail Price: $101.95
Low Price: $91.95

ADULT TRI-WHEEL BICYCLES

Schwinn Town and Country Tri-Wheeler Three-Speed

Best Buy

It's not easy finding a quality constructed adult tri-wheel bicycle at an affordable price, but this one fills the bill. It features the Schwinn Cantilever electro-forged steel frame construction in easy-on/easy-off ladies' style with semi-hi-rise handlebar of chrome-plated steel and black rubber safety grips. The gearing is differential-drive, three-speed hub with trigger control which is sure and easy to operate. The saddle is a comfortable Mesinger wide tourist style. There's an easily adjustable seat post, safety reflectorized pedals, and a full-length chainguard. Over the rear axle sits a detachable vinyl coated wire basket with handles for carrying parcels. The fenders are chrome-plated. There's a safety

parking brake, too. The tires are Schwinn Sports Touring, 24 × 1⅜ inches, mounted on Schwinn-built tubular steel rims. The weight is 65 pounds. Attention to safety, handling, and the addition of several convenient features—all offered at a competitive price—make this tri-wheeler a Consumer Guide® best buy.

Approximate Retail Price: $276.95
Low Price: Not Available

Murray Three-Wheeler 0-5953

This adult tri-wheel bicycle features

a ladies' style tubular steel butted frame and semi-hi-rise handlebar. The saddle is an oversized cushion-type with dual rear braces. There's a Shimano three-speed rear hub with differential drive and special twist-grip shifter and rear coaster brake. There's also a front side-pull caliper brake for sure, easy stopping. A large wire basket sits over the rear axle and provides a handly means for carrying groceries, luggage, etc. The tires are Dae Yung 24 × 1¾-inch blackwall mounted on tubular steel, chrome-plated rims. There's also a

Schwinn's Town and Country

Murray's Senior Cycle

full-length chainguard. Chrome-plated steel fenders round out the package. Available in Flamboyant Black Cherry. Partial assembly is required.

Approximate Retail Price: $249.96
Low Price: Not Available

CYCLE EXERCISERS

Schwinn ergoMETRIC Exerciser

This ergoMETRIC Exerciser is a stationary bicycle ergometer which permits a closely controlled, measured, and repeatable cycling program. When pedaling with the resistance control set at a specific level (there are 11 different settings possible), energy expenditure remains relatively constant over a wide range of pedal speeds (from 50 to 90 rpms). Both the program and the rider's reaction to the program can be easily charted. The unit includes a program chart as part of the console; it can be used to record the length of riding time, resistance load, and rpms. The instrument panel includes a timer, odometer, speedometer, and push-button activated pedal resistance control with dial settings. The Dynamometer is tested and rated. It features solid state electronic regulation. Available in attractive Harvest Gold finish. The weight is 73 pounds.

Approximate Retail Price: $682.00
Low Price: Not Available

Schwinn's ErgoMETRIC Exerciser

Schwinn Deluxe Exerciser

It's easy to enjoy the benefits of cycling year 'round while riding in the comfort of the home. This exerciser features easily adjustable saddle and handlebar (it can be adjusted without tools to fit nearly any rider). The pedals feature overshoe straps, and there's built-in pedal resistance to simulate an actual bicycle ride. The frame is built of tubular steel with wide base plates for firm, tip-free footing. A conveniently located control panel offers a speedometer, mileage indicator, timer, and adjustable pedal resistance control. The exerciser is equipped with semi-hi-rise handlebar and grips and mattress spring saddle. The weight is 56 pounds. The many thoughtful features and quality construction make this cycle exerciser a Consumer Guide® best buy. Available in attractive Harvest Gold finish. Also available: an exerciser reading stand with a non-glare flat black finish and chrome-plated support arms; this is easily installed and adjustable.

Approximate Retail Price: $196.95
Low Price: Not Available

Schwinn's Deluxe Exerciser

Prices are accurate at time of printing; subject to manufacturer's change.

Glossary Of Bicycling Terms

BICYCLE COMPONENT KEY

1. Brake lever
2. Handlebar, down-turned
3. Steering head
4. Caliper brake
5. Fork
6. Wheel hub
7. Rim
8. Tire
9. Spoke
10. Gear-shift lever
11. Down tube
12. Gear-shift cable
13. Toe strap
14. Pedal toe clip
15. Pedal
16. Crank
17. Chainwheel
18. Chain
19. Chain stay
20. Rear derailleur
21. Rear drop-out
22. Seat tube
23. Seat stay
24. Seat post
25. Seat (or saddle)
26. Top tube
27. Headset, top
28. Stem
29. Brake cable
30. Pump
31. Chain guide

Ankling: A method of pedaling in which the foot maintains pressure on the pedal all the way around the stroke.

Balloon Tire: Oversized, low-pressure tire usually found on single-speed coaster-brake bicycles.

Banana Seat: An elongated saddle with an added rear brace for support popular on children's bicycles.

Bar Plug: The handlebar end-plug for wrapped bars; it prevents the tape from unraveling.

Binder Bolt: The nut-and-bolt assembly that goes through the clamp that holds the handlebar to the gooseneck.

Bottom Bracket: The round tube containing the axle for the chainwheel and crank assemblies. Seat and downtubes are welded to this bracket, as are the bicycle's stays.

Brake Levers: The levers—either handlebar-, stem-,

or downtube-mounted—used to activate caliper brakes.

Brake Pads: The rubber "shoes" found on caliper brakes and used to grip the rim for stopping.

Cable: The twisted wire that runs to the caliper brakes and derailleurs.

Cage: The term given to the arms that hold the small wheels or rollers of the rear derailleur.

Caliper Brakes: Hand-operated brakes.

Chain: An articulated drive unit which transmits power from the chainwheel to the rear wheel.

Chain Stays: The frame tubes which go from the bottom bracket to where the rear wheel attaches to the frame; also called rear stays.

Chainwheel: The large geared wheel on the right side of the bottom bracket to which the crank is attached to drive the chain.

Clinchers: Tires that have separate tubes. The clincher tire is held to the rim by a bead that fits in the lip of the rim when the tire is inflated. The bead is formed by a wire encased in the casing. Also called wire-ons.

Coaster Brakes: Foot-activated internal-hub rear brakes.

Cotter Pin: A small pin used to hold the cranks on the bottom bracket axle in cottered-crank designs.

Cranks: The steel or aluminum alloy member attached to the chainwheel on the righthand side and to the axle on the lefthand side to which the pedals are attached.

Cyclometer: A device attached to the front fork which ticks off and measures elapsed mileage.

Derailleur: The device which moves the chain from one gear to another.

Derailleur Cage: The mechanism which holds the rear derailleur idler wheels.

Dishing: "Trueing" a derailleur-gear-equipped rear wheel so that the rim is centered over the axle and not over the hub. The wheel will appear to be right of the hub center (on the gear side).

Down Tube: That section of the frame which goes from the steering head to the bottom bracket.

Drop Outs: That section of the front fork (and of the rear chain stays) where the wheel or hub axle fits and to which the wheel axle is bolted.

Freewheel: The cluster of sprockets on the rear of a derailleur-equipped bicycle.

Fork Crown: The flat or slightly sloping part at the top of the fork, just beneath the steering head.

Front Fork: The part holding the front wheel drop outs which is turned by handlebars to steer the bicycle. Included in this unit is the steering-column fork crown (inside the head tube of the frame), the fork blades (round or oval, depending on whether the bike is a track or road model), and fork tips.

Front Drop Out: The lug brazed to the front fork bottom tips into which the front wheel axle fits.

Handlebar Stem: The steel piece, the top section of which holds the handlebars and the bottom section of which fits into the top of the fork.

Headset: The workings that hold the fork on the frame.

Head Tube: The short tube at the front of the frame in which the fork and stem join together.

Hub: The front or rear wheel unit which is drilled to receive the spokes and machined to hold the axle and bearings.

Jockey Sprocket: The top of the two rear derailleur idler wheels. This wheel moves the chain from one rear wheel gear to another.

Mudguards: Usually shortened fenders located from the top center of the wheel back.

Multispeed Hubs: Gears located in the rear hubs of non-derailleur-equipped geared bikes.

Pannier: A saddlebag for mounting on the rear of a bicycle, usually in pairs for balance. Smaller panniers are available for front-of-bicycle mounting.

Pawls: Pivoted arms that catch on the teeth to prevent movement.

Planet Gear: A gear-toothed wheel that revolves around and meshes with a center or sun gear.

Power Train: The system which includes the pedals, sprockets, chain, and the gears, if any.

Quick-Release Skewer: The mechanism to permit the quick removal of the front or rear wheels. Also called quick-release hubs.

Rattrap Pedals: All-steel racing and touring-style pedals.

Rear Drop Out: The lug that is brazed or welded to the seat stays and chain stays into which the rear wheel axle fits.

Rim: The wheel without spokes and hub; the device on which the tire is mounted.

Saddle: Seat.

Seat Cluster: A three-way lug into which is brazed or welded the top and seat tubes and seat stays.

Seat Post: The steel or aluminum alloy tube to which the seat is attached and which slips into the seat tube.

Seat Stays: The part of the frame extending from just under the seat to the rear wheel drop out.

Seat Tube: That frame member under the seat which is brazed to the bottom bracket and to the top tube.

Skewer: A quick-release device on racing-type wheel hubs which permits instant removal of the wheel.

Steering Head: The tube containing the fork cups and bearings, the stem, and the top section of the fork. Also called the headset.